To: Anglea & Trey

From: Granddaddy
Breedlove and
Billie

Christmas 2001

BILLY GRAHAM

The Secret
of Happiness

WORD PUBLISHING
Dallas London Vancouver Melbourne

Scripture, unless otherwise indicated, is from the
Authorized King James Version. Those marked RSV are from
the Revised Standard Version of the Bible, copyright 1946, 1952,
© 1971, 1973 by the Division of Christian Education of National
Council of the Churches of Christ in the U.S.A., and used
by permission. Quotations marked AMP are from
"The Amplified Bible," copyright © 1965 by
Zondervan Publishing House.

Book design by Mark McGarry
Set in Monotype Dante & ITC Syndor

Library of Congress Cataloging in Publication Data
Graham, Billy, 1918–
The secret of happiness

1. Beatitudes—Criticism, interpretation, etc.
2. Happiness—Religious aspects—Christianity.
I. Title. BT382.G7   1985   226'.9306   85–16934
ISBN 0–8499–0508–7
ISBN 0–8499–3034–0 (pbk.)
ISBN 0–8499–1478–7 (gift)

789012345   BVG   98765432
Printed in the United States of America

To my Mother and Father,
whose dedicated lives taught me
The Secret of Happiness

Contents

Preface

I SAT DOWN to write a book on "The Greatest Sermon Ever Preached"—the Sermon on the Mount—but I got no further than the eight Beatitudes. The more I read them, meditated on them and studied them, the more I realized that Christ was giving a formula for personal happiness that applied to anyone, no matter what his race, geographical situation, age or circumstance! I have based my comments on the beautiful and beloved King James Version of the Beatitudes, although I follow the suggestion of scholars and many modern Bible translations who use the word "happy" for "blessed" since it suggests joy in the midst of real life.

When trying to put these thoughts on paper, I consulted with other writers. In these few statements Jesus shares almost the whole depth and scope of His teaching. As someone has said, "The character which we find in the Beatitudes is beyond all question, nothing less than our Lord's own character put into words. It is a description set side by side with an example."

The Beatitudes are revolutionary! Startling! Deeply profound, and yet amazingly simple! If applied on a universal scale, they could transform the world in which we live.

If you apply these simple formulae in your own personal life, you can never be the same!

As I have restudied the Beatitudes to prepare for this revised edition I have been amazed again at the timelessness and universal nature of these teachings of Jesus. I have sensed afresh the depth and challenge of these brief words of our Lord. In this revised edition I have made numerous minor changes to bring the book up to date and make it practical. I also have included some additional insights which I have gathered since the first edition was published in 1955. But the Word of God does not change, nor does its power to change our lives. Just as Christ brought hope and new life to those who first gathered in Galilee to hear the Sermon on the Mount, so He can bring hope and new life to us today as we understand His truth, commit ourselves to it, and live each day in its light.

In the first edition, my friend and assistant Lee Fisher was a tremendous help. In this revised edition, my wife Ruth, my daughter Gigi Tchividjian, my able research assistant Dr. John Akers, and Word editor Al Bryant have been indispensable. I am deeply grateful also to my administrative assistant Stephanie Wills for her invaluable counsel, advice, and for keeping us on track.

It is my prayer that as you read this book, and as you meditate on the Beatitudes themselves, you will realize that these ancient truths are as modern as tomorrow. They can change your life and point the way to true and lasting happiness—because they will point you to Christ and His timeless principles for living.

One final note: I have used the word "man" in this book, along with the appropriate pronouns that follow it, in the generic sense of the term, to mean the human race in its most inclusive sense.

Billy Graham, Montreat, NC
August, 1985

Publisher's Note

SINCE ITS FIRST PUBLICATION over forty years ago, Dr. Billy Graham's *The Secret of Happiness* has offered inspiration to thousands in pursuit of this elusive goal. The eight guideposts Dr. Graham points to have helped us through decades of war, turmoil, and world change and have shown us how to maintain genuine happiness in their midst. While some world situations and statistics have changed since the book's most recent revision, our need to know the secret of happiness has not. Word Publishing is pleased, therefore, to join Dr. Graham in reaffirming the timeless truths found in the Beatitudes by republishing this devotional classic, as revised in 1985. May you be blessed as you continue your own search for true contentment and joy.

Blessed—happy, to be envied, and spiritually prosperous that is, with life-joy and satisfaction in God's favor and salvation, regardless of their outward conditions—are the poor in spirit. . . .   Matthew 5:3, AMP

CHAPTER ONE

The Search for Happiness

A FRENCH PHILOSOPHER once said, "The whole world is on a mad quest for security and happiness." A former president of Harvard University observed, "The world is searching for a creed to believe and a song to sing."

A Texas millionaire confided, "I thought money could buy happiness—I have been miserably disillusioned." A famous film star broke down: "I have money, beauty, glamour and popularity. I should be the happiest woman in the world, but I am miserable. Why?" One of Britain's top social leaders said, "I have lost all desire to live, yet I have everything to live for. What is the matter?"

The poet, Amy Wilson Carmichael, wrote:

> *The lonely, dreary road he trod.*
> *"Enter into my joy," said God.*

The sad ascetic shook his head,
"I've lost all taste for joy," he said.

A man went to see a psychiatrist. He said, "Doctor, I am lonely, despondent, and miserable. Can you help me?" The psychiatrist suggested that he go to a circus and see a famous clown who was said to make even the most despondent laugh with merriment. His patient said, "I am that clown."

A college senior said, "I am twenty-three. I have lived through enough experiences to be old, and I am already fed up with life."

A famous Grecian dancer of a generation ago once said, "I have never been alone but what my hands trembled, my eyes filled with tears, and my heart ached for a peace and happiness I have never found."

One of the world's great statesmen said to me, "I am an old man. Life has lost all meaning. I am ready to take a fateful leap into the unknown. Young man, can you give me a ray of hope?"

The Christian, on the other hand, has a different perspective on the meaning of happiness. C. S. Lewis said, "Joy is the serious business of heaven." He added, "All his biddings are joys." Mother Teresa of Calcutta says, "True holiness consists of doing the will of God with a smile."

Jesus declared, "I am come that they might have life, and that they might have it more abundantly" (John 10:10). Or again He stated, "These things have I spoken unto you, that my joy might remain in you, and that your joy might be full" (John 15:11).

Searching for Happiness in the Wrong Places

Over 2,500 years ago the prophet Isaiah looked out on a people who longed for happiness and security but were looking for it in the wrong places. They were running to the marketplace and to places of amusement, spending their money madly for things which brought them no permanent satisfaction.

He stood before them one day and gave them the Word of God: "Ho, every one that thirsteth, come ye to the waters, and he that hath no money: come ye, buy, and eat; yea, come, buy wine and milk without money and without price. Wherefore do ye spend money for that which is not bread? and your labor for that which satisfieth not? hearken diligently unto me, and eat ye that which is good, and let your soul delight itself in fatness" (Isaiah 55:1, 2).

Isaiah didn't speak negatively and berate them for their sins in this particular sermon. He didn't grab the bottle from the drunkard's hand, he didn't lecture them about the evils of gluttony, he didn't shame them for their immoral practices. He overlooked that for the moment. He simply asked them: "Are you getting what you want out of life? Why do you spend your money for that which is not bread and your labor for that which does not satisfy?"

If Isaiah were living today he would probably stand at Forty-second and Broadway in New York, in the Loop in Chicago, or on Market Street in San Francisco, and simply ask the milling, restless throngs: "Are you getting what you want? Are you finding satisfaction?"

He would ask the actress, surfeited with fame and fortune,

but peering out on life hungrily: "Are you getting what you want?" He would say to the eminently successful financier who commands his fleets and controls his industries: "Are you getting what you want?"

He would say to the laborers and workmen of America who are enjoying the highest standard of living in history: "Are you getting what you want?" He would ask the youth of America: "Are you getting what you want?"

He would say to the consumers of America who have the best homes, the most comfortable furniture, the finest food, the cleverest gadgets, and the smoothest, most powerful automobiles: "Are you getting what you want?"

God Has the Answer

Isaiah did not leave them with an unanswered question. He went on to tell them that there is a satisfying way of life, if they would seek it. He exhorted them to abandon their vain searching for pots of gold at the end of mythical rainbows, and to start searching for happiness where it is really found, in a right relationship with God.

Our materialistic world rushes on with its eternal quest for the fountain of happiness! The more knowledge we acquire, the less wisdom we seem to have. The more economic security we gain, the more bored and insecure we become. The more worldly pleasure we enjoy, the less satisfied and contented we are with life. We are like a restless sea, finding a little peace here and a little pleasure there, but nothing permanent and satisfying. So the search continues! Men will kill, lie, cheat, steal, and go to war to satisfy their quest for power, pleasure, and wealth, thinking thereby to gain for themselves and their particular group peace, security, contentment, and happiness, and yet in vain.

Yet inside us a little voice keeps saying, "We were not meant to be this way—we were meant for better things." We have a mysterious feeling that there is a fountain somewhere that contains the happiness which makes life worth while. We keep saying to ourselves that somewhere, sometime we will stumble onto the secret. Sometimes we feel that we have obtained it—only to find it illusive, leaving us disillusioned, bewildered, unhappy, and still searching.

There are, we need to realize, two kinds of happiness. One kind of happiness comes to us when our circumstances are pleasant and we are relatively free from troubles. The problem, however, is that this kind of happiness is fleeting and superficial. When circumstances change—as they inevitably do—then this kind of happiness evaporates like the early morning fog in the heat of the sun. In addition, even when our outward circumstances are seemingly ideal, we still may be troubled inside by a nagging hunger or longing for something we cannot identify. We say we are "happy"—but down inside we know it is only temporary and shallow at best. Yes, from time to time we may think we have found a degree of happiness, but sooner or later it will vanish. Our search for happiness remains unfulfilled.

But there is another kind of happiness—the kind for which we all long. This second kind of happiness is a lasting, inner joy and peace which survives in any circumstances. It is a happiness which endures no matter what comes our way—and even may grow stronger in adversity. This is the kind of happiness to which Jesus summons us in the Beatitudes. It is happiness which can only come from God. He alone has the answer to our search for lasting happiness.

The happiness which brings enduring worth to life is not the superficial happiness that is dependent on circumstances. It is the happiness and contentment that fills the soul even in the midst of the most distressing of circumstances and the most adverse environment. It is the kind of happiness that survives when things go wrong and smiles through the tears. The happiness for which our souls ache is one undisturbed by success or failure, one which dwells deep within us and gives inward relaxation, peace, and contentment, no matter what the surface problems may be. That kind of happiness stands in need of no outward stimulus.

Near my home is a spring that never varies its flow at any season of the year. Floods may rage near by, but it will not increase its flow. A long summer's drought may come, but it will not decrease. It is perennially and always the same. Such is the type of happiness for which we yearn.

The Three Things We Search For

First, we search for peace. As we have just seen, the whole human race is consumed with a search for inner peace, happiness, and joy.

The peace we seek is not merely a nondescript, so-called peace of mind which is blind to reality or comes and goes according to our moods or circumstances. The peace every man and woman seeks is one which will free them from the anxiety and frustrations of life's distracting conflicts and problems. It is a peace of soul which permeates one's entire being, a peace that operates through the trials and burdens of life.

Second, we search for purpose. Man is confused and perplexed, wondering where he came from, why he is here, and where he is going. He wants to know if there is truth in this universe—truth which will be like a polar star to guide him and give him meaning.

Some speculate that humanity is an accident on this planet. According to their views, man was not put here for a purpose—he just happened. The existentialist philosopher declares that man has no God-given purpose, and is left to make up his own purpose and meaning in life if he can. But down inside we yearn for something more certain. Even the skeptic searches for truth, for man needs truth as the animals do not—not just the truth of the physical sciences and mathematics, but the truth about his being and why he is here.

Third, we search for a relationship with God. Even when men vehemently deny God's existence, they still are searching for something to fill the vacuum in their souls.

But it is a vacuum God, our Creator, placed there—and only He can fill it. Man was created in the image of God. At first, Adam and Eve had perfect fellowship with God. But they turned their backs on God, substituting themselves at the center of their lives instead of God their Creator. Now man is a lost and lonely wanderer upon the earth apart from God. To have a vague knowledge that He exists is not enough. Man yearns to know that he is not alone in this universe, that there is a Higher Power guiding his destiny. He yearns for a relationship with his Creator—even if he does not admit it.

The Beatitudes: God's Key to Man's Search

Yes, every human being ever born yearns for peace, purpose, and God Himself. But can we know these? Can our search be ended? Will our quest for true happiness ever be satisfied? The Bible declares a resounding "Yes!" And in these eight Beatitudes Jesus points the way. In each one of the Beatitudes—which someone has called the "beautiful attitudes"—Jesus used the word *blessed*. This word *blessed is* actually a very difficult word to translate into modern English, because in the original Greek language of the New Testament it has a far richer meaning than the everyday content of our English word. As we noted at the beginning of this chapter, the Amplified Version of the New Testament defines it as "happy, to be envied, and spiritually prosperous . . . with life, joy and ,satisfaction. . . ." But perhaps the word "happy" comes as close as any single English word to conveying the idea of "blessed" to us today, and that is the word we will use for the most part through this book. But let us never forget that the "blessedness" of which Jesus speaks is far, far deeper than any superficial happiness which comes and goes according to circumstances. That is why the word "blessed" guards well against its reduction and perversion.

Jesus' first words were: "Happy are ye." In those three

words He was telling us that there *is* an answer to our search! We can know peace. We can know the truth about our lives. We can know God. And because of that, we can be blessed!

But is that possible, or is Jesus simply speaking some high-sounding words which have no substance? To answer that, look first of all at Jesus Himself. Certainly if anyone had genuine happiness and blessedness, it was Jesus—in spite of the controversy, abuse, and eventual injustice of His death. He knew the secret of true happiness, and in these Beatitudes He unveils it to us.

Who Was This Jesus?

The Beatitudes are not the whole of Jesus' teaching, nor is even the Sermon on the Mount. (You can read the entire Sermon on the Mount in chapters five through seven of the Gospel of Matthew.) There is much else that Jesus taught during the three short years of His public ministry. But Jesus was more than a great teacher. Who was this man Jesus, who never traveled outside His native Palestine and yet changed the entire course of human history?

Some have said that Jesus' main role was as a social reformer, coming to change society and liberate people who were bound by injustice and oppression. Others have said He came merely as an example, showing us by His acts of love how we should live. Still others have dismissed Him as a misguided religious reformer with no relevance to a modern, scientific age.

But none of these is adequate to explain Jesus Christ as

we see Him clearly pictured in the New Testament. The Bible, in fact, makes a startling assertion: Jesus was not only a man, but He was God Himself, come down from the glory of Heaven to walk on this earth and show us what God is like. Christ "is the image of the invisible God" (Colossians 1:15). More than that, He is the divinely appointed Savior who died for sinners, bearing their transgressions upon the cross. He died to save all who had disobeyed God and who were slandering Him in their unregenerate natures. And He demonstrated beyond all doubt that He was the Divine Savior and Lord by being raised from the dead. The gospel is the good news of God "concerning his Son Jesus Christ our Lord, which was made of the seed of David according to the flesh; And declared to be the Son of God with power, according to the spirit of holiness, by the resurrection from the dead" (Romans 1:3–4).

The best modern scholarship is discovering once again that even the Sermon on the Mount, and the Beatitudes as well, cannot be isolated from the fact of Jesus' saviorhood. The Old Testament had taught that the Christ was to be meek. He was to turn mourning into joy; righteousness was to be His meat and drink; even upon the cross it was His deepest hunger and thirst.

He also was the One who would show God's mercy to those who were separated from God and in need. He likewise would be pure and without sin. Most of all, He would not flee the persecution that would come His way, but would bring peace—peace with God, peace within the human heart, and peace on earth.

This is another way of saying that, in reality, Jesus Christ is the perfect fulfillment, example and demonstration of the Beatitudes. He alone, in the history of the human race, experienced fully what He tells us about the happiness and blessedness of life. What He tells us, He tells us as the Savior who has redeemed us and who is teaching His followers. But more than that, He is the One who gives us the power to live according to His teachings. Christ's message when He was upon the earth was revolutionizing and understandable. His words were simple yet profound. And they shook people. His words provoked either happy acceptance or violent rejection. People were never the same after listening to Him. They were invariably better or worse—better if they accepted Him, worse if they rejected Him. They either followed Him in love or turned away in anger and indignation. There was a magic in His gospel which prompted men and women to decisive action. As He clearly said, "He that is not with me is against me."

Men Right Side Up in an Upside-down World

The people who followed Him were unique in their generation. They turned the world upside down because their hearts had been turned right side up. The world has never been the same. History took a sharp turn for the better. People began to behave like human beings. Dignity, nobility, and honor followed in the wake of Christianity. Art, music, and science—sparked by this new interpretation of life's meaning—began to progress and develop. Mankind began at long last to resemble again the "image of God" in which he was created. Society began to feel the impact of the Christian influence. Injustice, inhumanity, and intolerance were dislodged by the tidal wave of spiritual power which was released by Christ. As F. W. Boreham once said, "The Carpenter of Nazareth has encouraged the goldsmiths of the ages." Virtually every significant social movement in Western Civilization—from the abolition of slavery to child labor laws—owes its origin to the influence of Jesus Christ.

Centuries have rolled by since that initial surge of spiritual life. The stream of Christianity has flowed unceasingly, sometimes at flood tide but more often at ebb tide.

At times the Church has been gloriously renewed and used of God. Emboldened by the Holy Spirit, and stirred by the truth of the Word of God, men and women throughout the centuries have continued to turn the world upside down for Christ. At other times, however, man-made tributaries have flowed into it, polluting and adulterating it. Deism, Pantheism, and, of late, Humanism and blatant Naturalism have flowed like muddy currents into the mainstream of Christian thought, so that the world has had difficulty in distinguishing the real from the false. In some parts of the world armies have fought and killed supposedly in the name of Christ—and yet by their actions showing they understood little of His spirit of forgiveness and love.

Yes, Christians are imperfect, and some who have claimed most loudly to follow Him have been the furthest from His teaching. But don't let that divert you or keep you from Christ Himself. At times people have said to me, "Christians are all hypocrites—I don't want anything to do with Christ!" But that is an excuse to keep from having to face the truth that is in Christ. Instead, understand His teaching and examine His life. And if you know Christ and have committed your life to Him, learn from Him and live a consistent life for Him. Do others see something of Christ—His love, His joy, His peace—in your life?

True Christians are supposed to be happy! Our generation has become well versed in Christian terminology, but is remiss in the actual practice of Christ's principles and teachings. Hence, our greatest need today is not more Christianity but more true Christians.

The Impact of Christlike Living

The world may argue against Christianity as an institution, but there is no convincing argument against a person who through the Spirit of God has been made Christlike. Such a one is a living rebuke to the selfishness, rationalism, and materialism of the day. Too often we have debated with the world on the letter of the law when we should have been living oracles of God, seen and read of all people.

It is time that we retrace our steps to the source and realize afresh the transforming power of Jesus Christ.

Jesus said to the woman at Jacob's well: "Whosoever drinketh of the water that I shall give him shall never thirst" (John 4:14). This sinsick, disillusioned woman was the symbol of the whole race. Her longings were our longings! Her heart-cry was our heart-cry! Her disillusionment was our disillusionment! Her sin was our sin! But her Savior can be our Savior! Her forgiveness can be our forgiveness! Her joy can be our joy!

An Invitation to a Journey

I invite you to go with me on a thrilling, adventuresome journey. The object of our search? The secret of happiness. The place? Galilee! Let us roll back the pages of time almost two thousand years.

It's a hot, sultry day with the sweltering wind spinning little dust whirls and carrying them swiftly down the winding road by the Sea of Galilee. There is an air of expectancy in the atmosphere we breathe. The wind skips happily across the surface of the ancient sea. We hear voices raised in an excited, feverish pitch as friend calls a greeting to friend. Along every trail leading to Galilee little groups of people begin to gather. The word has spread abroad that Jesus is returning to Galilee.

Suddenly He and His little band of followers emerge over the brow of a hill on the road to Capernaum, and immediately in their wake follows a vast multitude of people from Galilee, Decapolis, Jerusalem, Judea, and from beyond the Jordan River.

Quickly the word spreads from mouth to mouth: "Jesus is coming!" Other multitudes from Tiberias, Bethsaida, and Capernaum soon appear and join the others. Together they follow thirteen robed men. As they reach the summit of the hill where the gentle winds from the plains sweep over them, affording relief from the sun, Jesus stops and motions for them to sit down and rest.

The air is tense. It is a moment to be captured and held for eternity. The crowd hushes as Jesus climbs atop a large rock and is seated. In the valley on the deserted road, a lone camel rider wends his way along the trail toward Tiberias. A quiet falls upon the multitude as their faces gaze expectantly at Jesus. Then He begins to speak.

What He said there on that Mount of Beatitudes in faraway Palestine was to go down in history as the most profound, sublime words ever spoken! There in reverent, measured, simple words He revealed the secret of happiness—not a superficial happiness of time and space, but a happiness which would last forever.

His first word was "happy." Immediately His listeners must have pricked up their ears, as we are prone to do. In the pages to follow it is my prayer that you will do even more: prick up your ears . . . open your heart . . . surrender your will. Then you will begin living life with a capital L, find a contentment and joy that crowd the futility and vanity out of the daily walk, and discover the secret of happiness!

Blessed are the poor in spirit: for theirs is the
kingdom of heaven.   Matthew 5:3

CHAPTER TWO

Happiness through Poverty

TODAY, through the media, we have all been made aware of the abject, hopeless poverty in much of the world. We have seen the starving in Africa, the displaced persons of southeast Asia.

I myself have traveled in more than sixty countries of the world, many of them hopelessly buried in poverty. I have returned from cities like Calcutta with a heavy heart, wondering if anything can ever be done to alleviate their suffering.

Throughout the world I have found many Mother Teresas. Still, the poverty is virtually untouched. We have sent our own contributions through reliable relief organizations.

Yet under the filth, the starvation, the abject poverty I have sensed an even greater poverty—the poverty of the soul.

A French leader has said that if the whole world had

enough to eat, money to spend, and security from the cradle to the grave they would ask for nothing more. And that is something to think about. I have on occasion visited places where the wealthy gather to relax, escape bad weather, or just play—and I have discovered that wealth can be anesthetizing. It is, as Jesus said, easier for a camel to go through the eye of a needle than for a wealthy person to enter the kingdom of heaven (see Matthew 19:24). Surely one reason is that wealth tends to preoccupy a person and dull his sensitivity to his spiritual needs.

I have often asked myself the question: would wealth make people happy? And I have answered it just as quickly by saying an emphatic "No!" I know too many rich people who are miserable. There are people with everything that money can buy who are tormented, confused, bewildered, and miserable! Yet how many times I have heard people say, "If only I had a little security, I could be happy." Or, "If only I could have a fine home, a new car, and a winter condominium in Florida, I would be content."

There is nothing inherently wrong with being rich. I have been privileged to know some very wealthy people across the years who were humble and generous, seeing their wealth as a God-given means to help others. The Bible, however, warns that riches easily overwhelm a person, distorting his values, making him proud and arrogant, and making him think he does not need God. "But they that will be rich fall into temptation and a snare, and into many foolish and hurtful lusts, which drown men in destruction and perdition. For the love of money is the root of all evil" (1 Timothy 6:9–10).

For others, wealth only leads to boredom. King Solomon was unquestionably one of the wealthiest men who ever lived. In his search for happiness he tried everything—possessions, music, sex, great building projects, knowledge—but in the end he declared about them, "I have seen all the works that are done under the sun; and, behold, all is vanity and vexation of spirit" (Ecclesiasties 1:14). Only God could satisfy his deepest longings and give him true happiness.

On the other hand, many great people stay poor all their lives, either through choice (such as a missionary or a person who chooses to live modestly and give away money to help others) or through unavoidable circumstances. There are others, however, who go through life filled with resentment, jealousy, and bitterness because they want "just a little bit more." They may have enough to satisfy their legitimate needs, but instead of being thankful for what they have—which would make them unimaginably wealthy in the eyes of those in poorer nations—they are consumed by a desire for riches. They believe the key to happiness would be found in greater wealth.

But Jesus made it plain that happiness and contentment are not found in possessions or money. He stated that material things and riches do not in themselves bring happiness and peace to the soul.

Happy is that person who has learned the secret of being content with whatever life brings him, and has learned to rejoice in the simple and beautiful things around him.

In his Introduction to his *Anthology* on George MacDonald, C. S. Lewis says of MacDonald: "His resignation to poverty was at the opposite pole from that of a stoic. He appears to have been a sunny, playful man, deeply appreciative of all really beautiful and delicious things that money can buy, and no less deeply content to do without them." In *Annals of a Quiet Neighborhood* MacDonald said of himself, "Let me, if I may, be ever welcomed to my room in winter by a glowing hearth, in summer by a vase of flowers; if I may not, let me then think how nice they would be, and bury myself in my work. I do not think that the road to contentment lies in despising what we have not got. Let us acknowledge all good, all delight that the world holds, and be content without it."

An Unforgettable Day

On that day almost two thousand years ago there were undoubtedly many in that great throng who believed as many today believe—that the key to happiness is to be found in wealth and possessions. As they gathered to listen to Jesus, perhaps they wondered if His words could actually make any difference to them in their search for happiness—as you may wonder. It was soon clear to them, however, that His message was unique, for He was pointing another way to happiness—God's way. And it was a message which applied to every person.

The Sermon on the Mount was delivered to two distinct groups of people: the *multitude* and the *disciples of Christ*. We can therefore assume that it contains significance and meaning for both the disciples and the multitude, else Jesus would not have addressed it to both.

It gave the *disciples* a glimpse into the lofty spiritual Promised Land in which they were to live as the followers of Christ. It revealed the high ethical plane on which they were to live. It showed that to be a Christian was no mere child's play.

As for the *multitude,* the Sermon was an unveiling of what it actually meant to be a follower of Christ. Up to that time Jesus had been to them a fascinating and intriguing miracle worker. His person was magnetic, His manner winsome, His voice compelling. His entire being marked Him as a man of unusual power. He was a master teacher, a formidable debater, a compassionate healer—the gentlest and the sternest of men. Never had they heard anyone like Him.

These people, whose lives were monotonously humdrum in that unromantic faraway land, responded to this Galilean. To spend a day following Him through the villages where He healed the sick, blessed little children, and talked about the kingdom of God was a never-to-be-forgotten experience.

But on this particular day many who followed Him were to be surprised. Religion to them had been little more than superstition and meaningless ceremony. It little occurred to them that there was any relevance between religion and life. They had given up ever being happy; and if they ever knew the meaning of the word *happy,* they had forgotten it.

But Jesus was to put the words *blessed, joyful,* and *happy* back into their vocabularies—and even better, He was to put the words into their very hearts and lives. As Henry van Dyke's grand old hymn puts it: "Joyful, joyful, we adore Thee."

When Jesus opened His mouth, the first word to fall from His lips was "happy." This word means "blessed, contented, or highly favored." *Happy?* Could any word have been more incongruous? Those who listened that day were far from being blessed or happy. Subdued by the Roman Empire, they were conquered. Poor, dejected, ill-clad, and pawns of an alien government, their lives were without hope and expectation. Happy? How could the meager existence of their lives be highly favored, blessed, and contented?

The Nature of Poverty

Quickly on the heels of that first word followed five others: "Happy are the poor in spirit." If Jesus had omitted the last two words, they would have all rejoiced, for they were all poor—even if they would have been puzzled at how their grinding poverty could possibly make them happy. But Jesus said "the poor in spirit."

Wondering, they listened as He went on. Hidden in these seemingly cryptic words was the first foundational secret of happiness. At first it sounds like a contradiction. We usually think of people who are poor as being unhappy. But Jesus teaches that happiness can be found in spite of poverty.

What kind of poverty did Jesus have in mind? Did He mean those who had very little of this world's goods? No. Certainly they were included. But Jesus was speaking to persons of every type—rich or poor, sick or well, educated or uneducated, young or old. God is concerned about every person on this planet, and Jesus' words were addressed to all persons, in every circumstance, and in every generation. They are addressed to you and me today.

The True Meaning of Spiritual Poverty

What did Jesus mean by being "poor in spirit"? There are at least four dimensions to this crucial question.

FIRST: If we are to be poor in spirit, *we must be aware of our spiritual poverty.*

No man is more pathetic than he who is in great need and is not aware of it. Remember Samson? Standing there in the valley of Sorek, surrounded by the lords of the Philistines, ". . . he wist not that the Lord was departed from him" (Judges 16:20).

The pitiable thing about the Pharisees was not so much their hypocrisy as it was their utter lack of knowledge of how poor they actually were in the sight of God.

Jesus told a dramatic story about a man who had mistaken ideas concerning poverty and riches. This man, in a self-satisfied soliloquy, one night said: "Soul, thou hast much goods laid up for many years; take thine ease, eat, drink, and be merry" (Luke 12:19).

It had never occurred to him that the soul cannot subsist on goods and that the heart cannot be nourished by wine and food. Because of his stupidity and his attaching an undue importance to material things, God said: "Thou fool" (Luke 12:20). And to all those of every age who are tempted to reason falsely as he did, God said: "So is he that layeth up treasure for himself, and is not rich toward God (Luke 12:21).

Each of us has a body with eyes, ears, nose, hands, and feet. This body has certain legitimate desires and appetites: the appetite for food and drink, the appetite for sex, and the appetite for fellowship. Each of these has been given to us

23

by God, to be used as He intended. At the same time, they can be distorted and misused, eventually bringing sorrow and ruin to our lives.

But the Bible teaches that a person is more than just a body—each of us is actually a living soul! Our souls are created in the image of God. Just as our bodies have certain characteristics and appetites, so do our souls. The characteristics of the soul are personality, intelligence, conscience, and memory. The human soul or spirit longs for peace, contentment, and happiness. Most of all, the soul has an appetite for God—a yearning to be reconciled to its Creator and to have fellowship with Him forever.

In the world in which we live, we give most attention to satisfying the appetites of the body and practically none to the soul. Consequently we are one-sided. We become fat physically and materially, while spiritually we are lean, weak, and anemic. Or we spend enormous amounts of time and money on fad diets, expensive exercise machines, and health clubs. For many people, these things only demonstrate their preoccupation with the physical side of life. To be sure, our bodies have been given us by God, and we are to take care of them in every way possible. But even more important is taking care of our souls. The apostle Paul told Timothy, "Train yourself in godliness; for while bodily training is of some value, godliness is of value in every way, as it holds promise for the present life and also for the life to come" (1 Timothy 4:7–8, RSV).

The soul, created in the image of God, cannot be fully satisfied until it knows God in the proper way. Only God can resolve the deepest longings, desires, and appetites of the soul.

I may have the glamour of a movie queen or I may have the riches of a Texas millionaire and still not find happiness, peace, and contentment. Why? Simply because I have given attention to the body but not to the soul.

The soul actually demands as much attention as the body. It demands fellowship and communion with God. It demands worship, quietness, and meditation. Unless the soul is fed and exercised daily, it becomes weak and shriveled. It remains discontented, confused, restless.

Many people turn to alcohol or drugs to try to drown the cryings and longings of the soul. Some turn to a new sex experience. Others attempt to quiet the longings of their souls in other ways. But nothing but God ever completely satisfies, because the soul was made for God, and without God it is restless and in secret torment.

The First Step

The first step to God is a realization of our spiritual poverty. The poor in spirit do not measure the worth of life in earthly possessions, which fade away, but in terms of eternal realities, which endure forever. Wise is the man who openly confesses his lack of spiritual wealth and in humility of heart cries, "God, be merciful unto me, a sinner."

In God's economy, emptying comes before filling, confession before forgiveness, and poverty before riches. Christ said there is a happiness in that acknowledgment of spiritual poverty which lets God come into our souls.

Now, the Bible teaches that our souls have a disease. It is

worse than any dreaded cancer or heart disease. It is the plague that causes all the troubles and difficulties in the world. It causes all the troubles, confusions, and disillusionments in our own lives. The name of the disease is an ugly word. We don't like to use it. But it's a word that the psychiatrists are beginning to use once again. In our desire to be modern, we had almost forgotten it, but once again we are beginning to realize that it is the root of all man's troubles. It is *sin*.

We have sinned against our Creator. God is holy, righteous, and just. He cannot allow sin to enter His presence. Consequently, sin has come between God and us.

Now, there must be a confession that we have broken His laws and are willing to renounce our sins. We must acknowledge that without His fellowship life has no real meaning. This is not easy! All of us have pride, though it may be expressed in various ways. We do not like to confess that we are wrong or that we have failed. But God says: "All have sinned, and come short of the glory of God" (Romans 3:23). We must confess our sin as the first step to happiness, peace, and contentment!

This generation, encouraged by many second-rate philosophies, has tried in vain to live oblivious to God. The current resurgence of religion in the world is a mass confession that Humanism has failed. Like the Laodiceans of old, we have said, "I am rich, and increased with goods, and have need of nothing" (Revelation 3:17); but we have discovered that our riches, like our beauty, are only skin-deep and not sufficient to satisfy our eternal souls.

Let us face this fact: We came into the world with nothing, and we will leave it with nothing.

Where do we get the notion that our idea of success and God's are the same? You have written a book; you are a clever manager and promoter; you are a talented artist; you are independently wealthy; you have achieved fame and fortune. Without the gifts of intelligence, imagination, personality, and physical energy—which are all endowed by God—where would you be?

Are we not born poor? Do we not die poor? And would we not be poor indeed without God's infinite mercy and love? We came out of nothing; and if we are anything, it is because God is everything. If He were to withhold His power for one brief instant from us, if He were to hold in check the breath of life for one moment, our physical existence would shrivel into nothingness and our souls would be whisked away into an endless eternity.

Those who are poor in spirit recognize their creatureliness and their sinfulness—but more, they are ready to confess their sins and renounce them.

The Cure for Our Spiritual Disease

We have seen that the first dimension of "poor in spirit" is a realization of our spiritual poverty. But can our poverty be overcome? Yes! And that leads us to the second dimension of what Jesus meant by being "poor in spirit."

SECOND: If we are to be poor in spirit, *we must receive the riches that Christ has provided by His death and resurrection.*

Would it not be wonderful if we could find an absolute cure for the troubles of human nature? Suppose we could give a shot in the arm to the whole human race that would fill us with love instead of hate, with contentment instead of greed. This would immediately solve all the problems that the world faces at this moment.

Many years ago two Americans were crossing the Atlantic and on a Sunday night they were singing the hymn, "Jesus, Lover of My Soul." They were joined by a third party who had a very rich tenor voice. When the music stopped one of the Americans turned to the third party to ask if he had been in the Civil War. The man replied that he had been a Confederate soldier. Then he was asked if he was at a certain place on a certain night and the man replied, "Yes." And he said that a curious thing had happened that night. This hymn recalled it to his mind. "I was on sentry duty at the edge of the wood. It was dark and very cold. I was frightened because the enemy was supposed to be near. I felt homesick and miserable. About midnight, when everything was still, I was beginning to feel so weary I thought I could comfort myself by singing a hymn and I remembered this hymn. 'All my trust on Thee is stayed/all my help from Thee I bring./ Cover my defenseless head/with the shadow of Thy wing.' After I had sung those words, a strange peace came on me and through the long night I felt no fear."

"Well," said one of the men, "listen to my story. I was a Union soldier and I was in the woods that night with a party of scouts. I saw you standing in the woods. My men focused their rifles on you but when you began to sing, we listened. We could not fire and I told them to put down their rifles. We'll go home," I said.

Our daily papers and television newscasts record discontentment and unhappiness all over the world. They are the result of greed, ambition, lust, prejudice, and evil desire. If people could only be content in whatever state they find themselves; if they could love their fellow men regardless of the color of their skin or their station in life; if those who "have" would show compassion on the "have-nots"; if the greedy would give up their unholy ambition for power—would not this world be a different place in which to live?

Suppose, also, a cure could be found for the past mistakes, failures and sins of mankind. Suppose by some miracle all the past could be straightened out, all of life's tangles could be unraveled and the broken strings of life could be repaired. Such a cure would cause a world-wide stampede!

The most thrilling news in all the world is the fact that there is a cure! A medicine has been provided! People can be forgiven of all sin! The cobwebs that have collected in our lives can be removed!

The sin, confusion, and disillusionment of life can be replaced by righteousness, joy, contentment, and happiness. A peace can be imparted to the soul that is not dependent on outward circumstances. This cure was provided by Jesus Christ two thousand years ago on the cross of Calvary.

The cross has become a symbol in much of the Western world, misused by many rock stars and others who do not comprehend its significance.

The death of Christ on that first Good Friday was no mere accident. It was an act of a loving God to reconcile people to

Himself. Sin had come between us and God. We could not be happy and contented apart from God. Therefore, in loving grace God sent His Son to bear our sins and to take the penalty and judgment that we deserved.

However, God requires something of us. We must confess our spiritual poverty, renounce our sins, and turn by faith to His Son, Jesus Christ. When we do that, we are born again. He gives us a new nature. He puts a little bit of heaven down in our souls. Our lives change. Contentment, peace, and happiness come into our souls for the first time.

In my travels I have watched for lastingly contented and happy people. I have found such people only where Christ has been personally and decisively received. There is only one permanent way to have peace of soul that wells up in joy, contentment, and happiness, and that is by repentance of sin and personal faith in Jesus Christ as Savior.

Has such a moment come to your life? Have you had the experience of receiving Christ? It is not simply an emotional experience. It is a simple surrender of the will to Christ. Do you really want happiness? Then you will have to pay the price of humbling yourself at the foot of the cross and receiving Christ as Savior.

Our Dependence on God

We must know our spiritual poverty . . . we must turn to Christ in repentance and faith to receive His riches . . . but there is still more if we are to grasp the true meaning of being "poor in spirit."

THIRD: If we are to be poor in spirit, *we must be conscious of our dependence on God,* our spiritual bankruptcy.

Jesus said we must become like children before we can enter the kingdom of heaven. Children are dependents. That is to say, they depend upon their parents for protection and care. Because of their relationship and position they are not poor; but if it were not for their established relationship with their parents, they could be helpless and poor indeed.

When we come to Christ, a wonderful thing immediately happens to us: We become children of God! We become part of His family, as His sons and daughters! "As many as received him, to them gave he power to become the sons of God, even to them that believe on his name: Which were born, not of blood, nor of the will of the flesh, nor of the will of man, but of God" (John 1:12 13). In fact, the Bible uses the idea of "adoption" to illustrate this great fact. At one time we were alienated from God, with no rights or privileges. But in Christ we were adopted into His family (Ephesians 1:5–6). "For ye are all the children of God by faith in Christ Jesus" (Galatians 3:26).

As God's children, we are His dependents. The Bible says: "Like as a father pitieth his children, so the Lord pitieth them that fear him" (Psalm 103:13).

Dependent children spend little time worrying about meals, clothing, and shelter. They assume, and they have a right to, that all will be provided by their parents.

Jesus said: "Take no thought, saying, What shall we eat? or, What shall we drink? or, Wherewithal shall we be clothed?

. . . But seek ye first the kingdom of God . . . and all these things shall be added unto you" (Matthew 6:31, 33).

Because God is responsible for our welfare, we are told to cast all our care upon Him, for He cares for us (1 Peter 5:7). Because we are dependent upon God, Jesus said: "Let not your heart be troubled" (John 14:1). God says, "I'll take the burden—don't give it a thought—leave it to Me."

Dependent children are not backward about asking for things. They would not be normal if they did not boldly make their needs known.

God has said to His dependent children: "Therefore come boldly unto the throne of grace, that we may obtain mercy, and find grace to help in time of need" (Hebrews 4:16). God is keenly aware that we are dependent upon Him for life's necessities. It was for that reason that Jesus said: "Ask, and it shall be given you; seek, and ye shall find; knock, and it shall be opened unto you" (Matthew 7:7).

What is troubling you today? Is your heart burdened because of some problem which threatens to overcome you? Are you filled with anxiety and worry about some problem, wondering what will happen? Listen: as a child of God through faith in Christ, you can turn these over to Christ, knowing that He loves you and He is able to help you. At times He may take the problem away; other times He may give you strength to bear it. But you can rest in Him. "Have no anxiety about anything, but in everything by prayer and supplication with thanksgiving let your requests be made known to God. And the peace of God, which passes all understanding, will keep your hearts and your minds in Christ Jesus" (Philippians 4: 6–7, RSV).

Happy is the person who has learned the secret of coming to God daily in prayer. Fifteen minutes alone with God every morning before one starts the day can change our outlooks and recharge our batteries.

But all of this happiness and all of these unlimited benefits which flow from the storehouse of heaven are contingent upon our relationship to God. Absolute dependency and absolute yieldedness are the conditions of being His child. Only His children are entitled to receive those things that lend themselves to happiness; and in order to be His child, there must be the surrender of the will to Him.

We must admit we are poor before we can be made rich. We must admit we are destitute before we can become children by adoption.

When we realize that all our own goodness is as filthy rags in God's sight and become aware of the destructive power of our stubborn wills, when we realize our absolute dependence upon the grace of God through faith and nothing more, then we have started on the road to happiness.

We do not come to know God through works—we come to know Him by faith through grace. We cannot work our way toward happiness and heaven; we cannot moralize our way, we cannot reform our way, we cannot buy our way. Salvation comes as a gift of God through Christ.

Serving Christ

As God's children we are not just meant to sit back and selfishly enjoy our privileges. Instead, God wants to use us to serve Him and help others. But before we can do that something else must happen in our hearts if we are truly to know the full meaning of Jesus' words: "Happy are the poor in spirit."

FOURTH: If we are to be poor in spirit, *we must willingly deny ourselves that we might better serve Christ.*

The poor in spirit are those who are willing to sell out their stock in themselves and to do as Jesus said: "Deny himself, and take up his cross, and follow me" (Matthew 16:24).

Our modern philosophy of self-reliance and self-sufficiency has caused many to believe that man can make the grade without God. "Religion," they argue, "may be all right for certain emotional people, but you can't beat a man who believes in himself." For example, the Austrian neurologist and founder of psychoanalysis, Dr. Sigmund Freud, said that religion was the universal obsessional neurosis.

But alas, this self-confident generation has produced more alcoholics, more drug addicts, more criminals, more wars, more broken homes, more assaults, more embezzlements, more murders, and more suicides than any other generation that ever lived. It is time all of us, from the intellectuals on down, to begin to take stock of our failures, blunders, and costly mistakes. It is about time that we place less confidence in ourselves and more trust and faith in God.

The rich young ruler who came to Jesus was so filled with his piety, his riches, and his greed that he revolted when Jesus informed him that the price of eternal life was to "sell out" and come and follow Him. He went away sorrowfully, the Bible says, because he could not detach himself from himself. He found it impossible to become "poor in spirit" because he had such a lofty estimate of his own importance.

All around us are arrogance, pride, and selfishness: these are the results of sin. From the heavens comes a voice speaking to a tormented, bankrupt world: "I counsel thee to buy of me gold tried in the fire, that thou mayest be rich; and white raiment, that thou mayest be clothed, and that the shame of thy nakedness do not appear; and anoint thine eyes with eyesalve, that thou mayest see. . . . Behold I stand at the door, and knock: if any man hear my voice, and open the door, I will come in to him, and will sup with him, and he with me" (Revelation 3:18, 20).

Heaven in this life and heaven in the life to come is not on a monetary standard. Nor can flesh and blood find the door to the kingdom of heaven with its contentment, peace, joy, and happiness. Only those who are poor in spirit and are rich toward God shall be accounted worthy to enter there, because they come not in their own merit but in the righteousness of the Redeemer.

Someone has said, "A man's wealth consists not in the abundance of his possessions, but in the fewness of his wants." "The first link between my soul and Christ," said C. H. Spurgeon, "is not my goodness but my badness, not my merit but my misery, not my riches but my need."

"Happy are the poor in spirit: for theirs is the kingdom of heaven!"

*Blessed are they that mourn: for they
shall be comforted.*   Matthew 5:4

CHAPTER THREE

Happiness While Mourning

THERE COMES a time in our lives when good-natured, well-meant encouragement like "Hang in there, pal" and "Cheer up, friend" fail to hoist us out of the doldrums. Because our needs are deeper than psychological, such suggestions only seem to make keener our feeling of helplessness.

The truth is: Regardless of our cleverness, our achievements and our gadgets, we are spiritual paupers without God.

Christ's message was directed to one specific group—to the "poor," the poor in spirit. Christ said: "The Spirit of the Lord is upon me, because he hath anointed me to preach the gospel to the poor" (Luke 4:18). This did not mean that Christ's message was only for the financially poor, the socially poor, or the intellectually poor. It meant that it was for those who recognized their spiritual poverty. That was the first Beatitude. It was the dominant note upon which this

37

celestial anthem of truth was composed. Of the Macedonian Christians Paul wrote, ". . . in a great trial of affliction the abundance of their joy and their deep poverty abounded unto the riches of their liberality" (2 Corinthians 8:2).

If we would find genuine happiness, we must begin where Jesus began. If we would have meaningful lives we must live by the Beatitudes.

This second Beatitude, "Happy are they that mourn," at first seems paradoxical. Do crying and joy go together? How can we possibly be happy while we are in the throes of mourning? How can one extract the perfume of gladness from the gall of sorrow?

But rest assured that there is deep and hidden significance here, for remember, Jesus was speaking to all people of all beliefs and of all ages and was revealing to them the secret of happiness.

The Shallowness of Our Lives

This present age is definitely not an age of mourning. Instead, people deliberately turn away from anything unpleasant, determined to fill their lives with those things which will divert their minds from anything serious. In their preoccupation with momentary pleasures and diversions, people settle for shallow and empty substitutes for reality. Millions give more thought to what programs they will watch tonight on TNT or what videotape they will rent for the weekend than they do to the things of eternity.

This century could well go down in history not so much

as a century of progress but as "the century of superficial-ity." The popular exclamation "So what!" aptly describes the attitude of many toward life. Many think that so long as we have sleek automobiles to ride in, TV and movies to enter-tain us, luxurious homes to live in, and a million gadgets to serve us, what happens to our souls does not matter. "So what! Laugh, and the world laughs with you; weep, and you weep alone." The apostles of mirth therefore put on their grimacing masks, turn the volume up on their TVs or press down the accelerators on their sports cars, and plunge into their superficial living.

But superficial living will never help us stand against the pressures and problems of life. At the end of the Sermon on the Mount Jesus told the story of two men. One decided to build his house on sand; it would, after all, have been easy to do. The other built his house on rock, although that would have involved more work. Outwardly both houses looked the same. But when the storms and floods came the house built on sand was destroyed. Only the house built on rock withstood the pressures of the flood. "Therefore whosoever heareth these sayings of mine, and doeth them, I will liken him unto a wise man, which built his house upon a rock" (Matthew 7:24). Only when our lives are grounded in the eternal truth of God's Word will they be able to withstand the storms of life. A superficial life which neglects God can never give us a firm foundation for true happiness.

The following comment appeared in an issue of *The Lon-don Times:* "The grace of final perseverance is that quality of patience that is always equal to the pressure of the passing moment, because it is rooted in the Eternal over which the passing moment has no power."

Beverly Sills, the former opera star and now a producer, has learned some lessons in adversity. Her first child was born almost totally deaf. The little girl was destined never to hear her mother's beautiful voice lifted in song. Her second child, a son, was born mentally retarded.

So great was the sorrow in Mrs. Sills' life that she took off a year from her demanding profession to work with her daughter and son, trying to make peace with the difficult circumstances. Later, when she was asked how she came to terms with the situation she answered, "The first question you ask is, Why me? Then it changes to Why them? It makes a complete difference in your attitude." Her attitude is the opposite of superficiality.

Now, I am not gunning for TV addicts or movie buffs in particular, but I do strongly contend that life is more than "skin-deep." Look at your popular comedians! Underneath the feigned smirks and the pretended smiles are the furrows and lines of seriousness and sobriety. Although it is their business to make you laugh, they are well aware that life is a solemn business.

Recently a dear friend of ours was told she had cancer. "It is amazing," she said to us, "how one day you can be going along smoothly and the next day one little word from the doctor's lips—'cancer'—radically changes everything. Then you know as you never have before that life is serious, and eternity is only a heartbeat away. Suddenly many of the things that seemed so important just a day ago are no longer very important."

Jesus did not mean "Blessed are the morose, the miserable, or the sullen." The Pharisees made a masquerade of religion, rubbed ashes on their faces to appear religious, but He strongly rebuked them for that. "Be not, as the hypocrites, of a sad countenance," He said (Matthew 6:16).

Who was it that said, "Some people's religion is like a man with a headache—he can't afford to give up his head, but it hurts him to keep it"?

The Meaning of Mourning

What did Jesus mean when He said: "Happy are they that mourn"? Certainly He did not mean to imply that a special blessing is promised to "crybabies," "weeping Willies," or the emotionally upset. This verse was not intended to be a comfort for abnormal psychopathic cases, which have somehow become mentally warped and take a morbid view of life. No, it was addressed to normal, average people for the purpose of showing them how to live happier, fuller, richer lives.

Let us begin with the word *mourning* itself. It means "to feel deep sorrow, to show great concern, or to deplore some existing wrong." It implies that if we are to live life on the higher plane then we are to be sensitive, sympathetic, tenderhearted, and alert to the needs of others and the world.

Perhaps we can see its meaning more clearly by thinking about its opposite. What is the opposite of mourning? Some might say it would be joy—and that is correct to a certain degree. But more than that, *the opposite of mourning is*

41

insensitivity, lack of caring, unconcern, callousness, indifference.
When I mourn it is because my heart has been touched by
the suffering and heartache of others—or even by my own
heartache. When I do not care and am indifferent, then I do
not mourn. The person who mourns is a person with a ten-
der and sensitive heart.

Kinds of Mourning

Let's list just six kinds of mourning which I believe were
implied in this most significant saying of our Lord. The word
here employed by Jesus covers such a wide range of attitudes that five shades of meaning are implied. We should
ponder each one of them prayerfully.

First, there is *the mourning of inadequacy.* Jeremiah, the
weeping prophet who mourned not in self-pity but for a
wayward, lost world, said: "O Lord, I know that the way of
man is not in himself: it is not in man that walketh to direct
his steps" (10:23).

Now, before I can become strong, I must first realize that
I am weak. Before I can become wise, I must first realize
that I am foolish. Before I can receive power, I must first confess that I am powerless. I must lament my sins before I can
rejoice in a Savior. Mourning, in God's sequence, always
comes before exultation. Blessed are those who mourn their
unworthiness, their helplessness, and their inadequacy.

Isaiah, the mighty prophet of God, knew by experience
that one must bow the knee in mourning before one can lift
the voice in jubilation. When his sin appeared ugly and ven-

omous in the bright light of God's holiness, he said: "Woe is me! for I am undone; because I am a man of unclean lips . . . for mine eyes have seen the King, the Lord of hosts" (Isaiah 6:5).

We cannot be satisfied with our goodness after beholding the holiness of God. But our mourning over our unworthiness and sinfulness should be of short duration, for God has said: "I, even I, am he that blotteth out thy transgressions for mine own sake, and will not remember thy sins" (Isaiah 43:25).

Isaiah had to experience the mourning of inadequacy before he could realize the joy of forgiveness. If I have no sense of sorrow for sin, how can I know the need of repentance?

In God's economy, a person must go down into the valley of grief before he or she can scale the heights of spiritual glory. One must become tired and weary of living without Christ before he or she can seek and find His fellowship. One must come to the end of "self" before one can really begin to live.

The mourning of inadequacy is a weeping that catches the attention of God. The Bible says: "The Lord is nigh unto them that are of a broken heart; and saveth such as be of a contrite spirit" (Psalm 34:18).

We have received hundreds of letters from people who tried desperately to "get hold of themselves," who in their own strength tried to shake off their habits, their sins, and their nasty dispositions—but all in vain. Finally in desperation they came to Christ, and in Him they found strength to be more than conquerors.

Experience reveals that we are inadequate. History proves that we are inadequate. The Bible declares that a person is inadequate to save himself. Christ's coming to the world proves the inadequacy of the race.

The happiest day of my life was the day I realized that my own ability, my own goodness, and my own morality were insufficient in the sight of God and I publicly and openly acknowledged my need of Christ. I am not exaggerating when I say that my mourning was turned to joy and my sighing into singing.

Happy are they who mourn for the inadequacy of self, for they shall be comforted with the sufficiency of God.

The Mourning of Repentance

Another kind of mourning is *the mourning of repentance*. Following the consciousness that we are inadequate comes the awareness of the reason for our insufficiency—sin. As individuals we have no control over the fact of sin in the universe, but as creatures of choice we are responsible for its presence in our lives. Because "all have sinned, and come short of the glory of God" (Romans 3:23), all need to mourn the fact of sin in their lives.

One technique of modern psychoanalysis is the association of present conflicts with past experiences. Sometimes when patients of psychiatry confess to past sins, they experience a certain release from their feelings of guilt. But since psychiatry is a science of the mind, it can do nothing for the soul. Only Christ is the Physician of the soul.

God has said: "Turn ye even to me with all your heart . . . with weeping, and with mourning" (Joel 2:12).

The mourning of repentance is not the weeping of self-pity; it is not regret over material losses nor remorse that our sins have been found out. It is entirely possible to be deeply sorry because of the devastation which sin has wrought in our lives—and yet not repent. I have had people pour out their hearts to me with tears, because their sins have been discovered and they are in serious trouble. But true repentance is more than being sorry for our sins and regretting the way we have allowed sin to shatter our lives. True repentance is a turning *from* sin—a conscious, deliberate decision to leave sin behind—and a conscious turning *to God* with a commitment to follow His will for our lives. It is a change of direction, an alteration of attitudes, and a yielding of the will. Humanly speaking, it is our small part in the plan of salvation—although even the strength to repent comes from God. But even so, the act of repentance does not win us any merit or make us worthy to be saved—it only conditions our hearts for the grace of God.

The Bible says: "Repent ye therefore, and be converted, that your sins may be blotted out, when the times of refreshing shall come from the presence of the Lord" (Acts 3:19). Our part is repenting. God will do the converting, the transforming, and the forgiving.

It will not be easy to bend our warped, stubborn wills; but once we do, it will be as though a misplaced vertebra has snapped back into place. Instead of the stress and tension of a life out of harmony with God will come the serenity of reconciliation. Our nerves will sense that our minds and hearts are relaxed, and they will send this happy news over their network to every fiber of our bodies: "Old things are passed away; behold all things are become new" (2 Corinthians 5:17).

Just as pain precedes birth, mourning over sin comes before spiritual rebirth. I do not mean to imply that in everyone's experience there will be loud, violent weeping over the sin in one's life—sorrow for sin may come quietly, with little or no emotion. But there will be a sincere sorrow for the evils of one's life and a disposition to turn to God for help and salvation. The Bible says: "For godly sorrow worketh repentance" (2 Corinthians 7:10).

The Mourning of Love

There is yet another aspect of this Beatitude, "Happy are they that mourn." There is, third, *the mourning of love.*

In many of the older cars the fuel gauge used to contain a red liquid, and its level in the gauge corresponded to the level of fuel in the tank. As the liquid was in the gauge, so it was in the tank.

If I would know the measure of my love for God, I must simply observe my love for people around me. My compassion for others is an accurate gauge of my devotion to God.

The Bible puts it this way: "Let us love one another: for love is of God; and every one that loveth is born of God, and knoweth God. . . . And this commandment have we from him, That he who loveth God love his brother also" (1 John 4:7, 21).

Some time ago, with some friends, I went through a museum in San Francisco. Among other things, we saw a collection of instruments of torture which were employed by religious people to force other people to believe as they did. History is largely the record of man's inhumanity to man.

This age in which we live could hardly be described as one in which people are honestly sensitive to the needs of others. We have developed a veneer of sophistication—but also cynicism and hardness. Our popular music talks constantly about love, and yet divorce rates skyrocket, child abuse is rampant, and our world is shaken by wars, violence, and terrorism. Major news magazines feature cover stories on "The 'Me' Generation." This generation, it seems, would rather see a prizefight than fight for a prize. Not only has the song "Rescue the perishing, care for the dying" disappeared from most of our songbooks, its theme has disappeared from our hearts, except for physical famine, victims of oppressive regimes and tidal waves. And these are terribly important. It is just that the spiritually perishing need to hear the gospel.

Several years ago we were visiting India. While we were there a terrible tidal wave hit a fifty-mile section of the coast, killing tens of thousands of people and completely destroying hundreds of villages and towns. Indian officials graciously provided a helicopter and accompanied us to the area, and we were among the first to view the devastation. I will never forget the terrible destruction and the stench of death—as if a thousand atom bombs had gone off at the same time. And yet this terrible disaster rated only a few inches in many American newspapers and only a minute or so on the evening news.

THE SECRET OF HAPPINESS

Abraham Lincoln once said, characteristically: "I am sorry for the man who can't feel the whip when it is laid on the other man's back."

Much of the world is callous and indifferent toward mankind's poverty and distress. This is due largely to the fact that for many people there has never been a rebirth. The love of God has never been shed abroad in their hearts.

Many people speak of the social gospel as though it were separate and apart from the redemptive gospel. The truth is: There is only one gospel. Divine love, like a reflected sunbeam, shines down before it radiates out. Unless our hearts are conditioned by the Holy Spirit to receive and reflect the warmth of God's compassion, we cannot love our fellow men as we ought.

Jesus wept tears of compassion at the graveside of a friend. He mourned over Jerusalem because as a city it had lost its appreciation of the things of the spirit. His great heart was sensitive to the needs of others.

To emphasize the importance of people's love for each other, He revised an old commandment to make it read: "Thou shalt love the Lord thy God with all thy heart . . . and thy neighbor as thyself" (Luke 10:27).

St. Francis of Assisi had discovered the secret of happiness when he prayed:

> *O Divine Master, grant that I may not so much seek*
> *To be consoled as to console,*
> *To be understood as to understand,*
> *To be loved as to love;*

For it is in giving that we receive;
It is in pardoning that we are pardoned;
It is in dying that we are born to eternal life!

This generation is rough and tough. I heard a little boy boasting one day about how tough he was. He said, "On the street I live on, the farther out you go the tougher they get, and I live in the last house."

Tears shed for self are tears of weakness, but tears of love shed for others are a sign of strength. I am not as sensitive as I ought to be until I am able to "weep o'er the erring one and lift up the fallen." And until I have learned the value of compassionately sharing others' sorrow, distress, and misfortune, I cannot know real happiness.

The Mourning of Soul Travail

Another kind of mourning which brings comfort is, fourth, *the mourning of soul travail.*

This may seem cryptic, but it represents a very real and a profitable kind of mourning. The Bible says: "As soon as Zion travailed, she brought forth her children" (Isaiah 66:8).

We don't use this phrase "soul travail" very often, not as much as our spiritual forefathers a generation or so ago. "'Travail" means "toil, painful effort, labor." "Travail of soul" therefore means spiritual toil—not necessarily outward labor which others will see, but that which takes place within the secret recesses of our souls. It refers to the continual flow of prayer which rises out of the Christian heart for a world which is spiritually unborn. And don't be under any illusions: this kind of soul travail is difficult and costly, because we are involved in spiritual warfare against Satan, the Enemy of Souls. "Pray without ceasing," the Bible says (1 Thessalonians 5:17).

God has worked in a miraculous way in our crusades down through the years. Thousands of men and women have made their decisions for Christ. Their coming was not the result of one man's work or the efforts of a group of men— it was the product of much prayer by many people around the world. God has said: "If my people . . . pray . . . then will I hear from heaven" (2 Chronicles 7:14).

Before three thousand people were brought into the Church on the day of Pentecost, the disciples had spent fifty days in prayer, fasting, and spiritual travail.

John Knox, with an all-consuming soul-concern for his country prayed: "Give me Scotland, or I die!" His earnest travail was rewarded with a spiritual rebirth in his land. This is what is termed "praying in the Spirit." It is the manifestation of a deep spiritual concern for others, and it is instilled by the Spirit of God.

The Bible says: "For we know not what we should pray for as we ought: but the Spirit itself maketh intercession for us with groanings which cannot be uttered" (Romans 8:26).

This kind of prayer can span oceans, cross burning deserts, leap over mountains, and penetrate jungles to carry the healing, helping power of the gospel to the objects of our prayer.

This kind of mourning, this quality of concern, is produced by the presence of God's Spirit in our lives. That "the

Spirit itself maketh intercession" indicates that it is actually God pleading, praying, and mourning through us. Thus we become co-laborers with God, actual partners with Him: our lives are lifted from the low plane of selfishness to the high plane of creativeness with God.

John Knox travailed in prayer, and the Church in Scotland expanded into new life. John Wesley travailed in prayer, and the Methodist movement was born. Martin Luther travailed, and the Reformation was under way.

God desires that we Christians be concerned and burdened for a lost world. If we pray this kind of prayer, an era of peace may come to the world and hordes of wickedness may be turned back. "As soon as Zion travailed, she brought forth her children" (Isaiah 66:8).

The Mourning of Suffering and Bereavement

Another kind of mourning we shall deal with is, fifth, *the mourning of bereavement.*

Nowhere has God promised anyone, even His children, immunity from sorrow, suffering, and pain. This world is a "vale of tears," and disappointment and heartache are as inevitable as clouds and shadows. Suffering is often the crucible in which our faith is tested. Those who successfully come through the "furnace of affliction" are the ones who emerge "like gold tried in the fire."

The Bible teaches unmistakably that we can triumph over bereavement. The Psalmist said: "Weeping may endure for a night, but joy cometh in the morning" (Psalm 30:5).

Self-pity can bring no enduring comfort. The fact is, it will only add to our misery. And unremitting grief will give us little consolation in itself, for grief begets grief. Ceaseless grieving will only magnify our sorrow. We should not peddle our sorrows and bewail our bad fortune—that will only depress others. Sorrow, or mourning, when it is borne in a Christian way, contains a built-in comfort. "Blessed are they that mourn: for they shall be comforted" (Matthew 5:4).

There is comfort in mourning *because we know that Christ is with us.* He has said: "Lo, I am with you alway, even unto the end of the world" (Matthew 28:20). Suffering is endurable if we do not have to bear it alone; and the more compassionate the Presence, the less acute the pain.

How often when a child have you stubbed your toe, bruised a leg, or cut a hand, and, running to the arms of your mother, you there sobbed out your pain? Lovingly caressing you and tenderly kissing the hurt, she imparted the magic of healing; and you went your way half healed and wholly comforted. Love and compassion contain a stronger balm than all the salves and ointments made by man.

Yes, when a loved one dies it is natural for us to feel a sense of loss and even a deep loneliness. That will not necessarily vanish overnight. But even when we feel the pain of bereavement most intensely, we can also know the gracious and loving presence of Christ most closely. Christ—who suffered alone on the cross, and endured death and hell alone for our salvation—knows what it is to suffer and be lonely. And because He knows, He is able to comfort us by His presence. "Blessed be God, even the Father of our Lord Jesus

Christ, the Father of mercies, and the God of all comfort; Who comforteth us in all our tribulation, that we may be able to comfort them which are in any trouble, by the comfort wherewith we ourselves are comforted of God" (2 Corinthians 1:3–4).

So, in our lives, there can be a blessedness in the midst of mourning. From suffering and bereavement God can bring into our lives new measures of His strength and love.

Jesus said, "Let not your heart be troubled . . . believe . . . in me" (John 14:1). When faith is strong, troubles become trifles.

There is also comfort in mourning *because in the midst of mourning God gives a song.* God says in Job 30:9: "I am their song." In Job 35:10 Elihu asks, "Where is God my maker, who giveth songs in the night?" His presence in our lives changes our mourning into song, and that song is a song of comfort. Sometimes it must be night to have that song!

This kind of comfort is the kind which enabled a devout Englishman to look at a deep, dark hole in the ground where his home stood before the bombing and say, "I always did want a basement, I did. Now I can jolly well build another house like I always wanted."

This kind of comfort is the kind which enabled a young minister's wife in a church near us to teach her Sunday school class of girls on the very day of her husband's funeral. Her mourning was not the kind which had no hope—it was a mourning of faith in the goodness and wisdom of God; it believed that our Heavenly Father makes no mistakes.

In addition, there can be comfort in mourning *because God*

can use our sufferings to teach us and make us better people. Often it takes suffering to make us realize the brevity of life, and the importance of living for Christ. Often God uses suffering to accomplish things in our lives that would otherwise never be achieved.

The Bible puts it succinctly: "Count it all joy, my brethren, when you meet various trials, for you know that the testing of your faith produces steadfastness. And let steadfastness have its full effect, that you may be perfect and complete, lacking in nothing" (James 1:2–4, RSV). Some of the godliest people I have ever known were men and women who had been called upon to endure great suffering—perhaps even being invalids for many years. Many people would have grown bitter and resentful if they had faced such circumstances—and yet because they knew Christ and walked in the joy of His presence every day, God had blessed them and turned them into people who reflected Christ. Often I have gone into a sickroom or hospital room to encourage someone—and have left feeling I was the one who had been encouraged and helped, because God had used their trials to make them more like Christ.

Before the power of the atom was discovered, science had to devise a way to "smash" the atom. The secret of the atom's immeasurable and limitless power was in its being crushed.

Dr. Edward Judson, at the dedication of the Judson Memorial Church in New York City, said, "Suffering and success go together. If you are succeeding without suffering, it is because others before you have suffered; if you are suffering without succeeding, it is that others after you may succeed."

Most of all, there is comfort in mourning *because we know that this life is not all, but we have the hope of Heaven.* Paul said, "If in this life only we have hope in Christ, we are of all men most miserable" (1 Corinthians 15:19). But he knew that our hope was not just in this life, but in Heaven. Our hope is in the resurrected Christ who has opened the door to eternal life for all who put their trust in Him. "O death, where is thy sting? O grave, where is thy victory? . . . thanks be to God, which giveth us the victory through our Lord Jesus Christ" (1 Corinthians 15:55, 57).

I will never forget the last few months of my mother's life, just before she went to be with the Lord. During those months she grew weaker and weaker physically—but her joy and excitement about heaven grew stronger and stronger! Whenever anyone went to visit her they came away marveling at her radiance and sense of expectancy. Yes, when she died there were tears—but in the midst of them, those of us who loved her had a deep sense of joy and comfort because we knew she was with the Lord. "Happy are they that mourn, for they shall be comforted."

This was the apostle Paul's hope—a hope based squarely on the fact of Jesus' resurrection. "We are troubled on every side, yet not distressed. . . . though our outward man perish, yet the inward man is renewed day by day. For our light affliction, which is but for a moment, worketh for us a far more exceeding and eternal weight of glory; While we look not at the things which are seen, but at the things which are not seen; for the things which are seen are temporal; but the things which are not seen are eternal" (2 Corinthians 4:8,

16–18). Jesus declared, "I am the resurrection, and the life: he that believeth in me, though he were dead, yet shall he live: And whosoever liveth and believeth in me shall never die" (John 11:25–26).

Do you have that hope in your heart? Do you know that if you were to die tonight you would go to heaven to be with Christ forever? You can, if you will trust Christ as your personal Savior and Lord. Jesus promised, "I go to prepare a place for you. . . . that where I am, there ye may be also" (John 14:2-3).

"Blessed (happy) are they that mourn." They are happy because they know that their aim, their distress, and their privation are the travail of a new creation, the birth pangs of a better world. They are happy because they are aware that the Master Artist—God—is employing both light and shadow to produce a masterpiece worthy of divine artistry. They are also made to glory in their infirmities, to smile through their tears, and to sing in the midst of their sorrow because they realize that in God's economy "if we suffer, we shall also reign with him" (2 Timothy 2:12).

The Mourning of Blank Despair

Lastly, there is *the mourning of blank despair*. "I could not think about my own death," says one young AIDS victim. "I wanted to live forever."

The tragedy of AIDS is obvious. But as C. S. Lewis said of war, "War does not increase death. Death is total in every generation." So it could be said of AIDS; it does not increase death; death is total in every generation.

However, in this present grim situation, a merciful God has given people time. A short time perhaps, torn with frustration, anger, bitterness and fear—but still time. Time to think of God, His love for a world gone wrong, the sending of His Son to bear in His own body on the cross, all the sins of mankind. Time to come to Him in childlike repentance and to discover the love of Jesus, His transforming power, and the life everlasting that He promises and has gone to prepare for us.

Blessed are the meek: for they shall inherit the earth.   Matthew 5:5

CHAPTER FOUR

Happiness through Meekness

MOST OF US seek short cuts to happiness. We search for the gold nuggets of spiritual satisfaction on the surface instead of in the depths, where they are found in abundance. It is only natural to follow the line of least resistance, forgetting all the while that heat and light are both products of resistance, a resistance which releases the latent forces of life.

Many of us are like the man out West who had a junk yard. He labored hard and long, buying and selling the old salvage he gathered from the back alleys of the city. But one day he discovered that his junk yard was located on an oil field. He hired a drilling crew, and soon the black gold flowed abundantly from the bosom of the earth. His junk yard was transformed into a veritable mine of wealth which knew no limits.

In these Beatitudes we have a mine of spiritual gold. To many it seems too good to be true, so they go their way, scratching around on the surface of life, picking up salvage in the form of gadgets, gold, and gimmicks. Because they ignore the challenge and the promise of these secrets of happiness, they miss the key to radiant living and remain spiritual paupers, submerged in a misery of their own making.

They forget that what happens *within* them is more important than what happens *to* them. Because they have built no inner fortifications, they fall a prey to the Enemy. They become filled with resentments and are baffled by frustration and depressed by disillusionment.

Would God have bothered to send His Son to the world if we had been able to face life and eternity alone? Christ's coming to the world proved that God was not happy with our unhappiness. He sent Him not only that we might have eternal life but that we might have life here and now, and that we might have it more abundantly—Life with a capital L!

Jesus' teaching was unique and different. He took religion out of the theoretical realm and placed it in the practical. He used no qualifying statements or phrases in declaring His way of life. He didn't use such phrases as "I venture to say" or "Perhaps it's this way" or "It is my considered opinion."

He spoke with authority! He spoke with finality! He spoke as though He knew . . . and He did! When the Sermon on the Mount was completed we read that "the people were astonished at his doctrine: for he taught them as one having authority, and not as the scribes" (Matthew 7:28–29).

His was not the soft, empty conjecture of the philosopher who professes to search for truth but readily admits he has never found it. It was more the confident voice of the mathematician who gives his answers unhesitatingly because the proof of the answer can be found within the problem.

He taught with authority because He was more than just another religious teacher—He was God Himself, who had come down in human flesh. His words are true, because He is God and God cannot lie. "God . . . hath in these last days spoken unto us by his Son, whom he hath appointed heir of all things, by whom also he made the worlds" (Hebrews 1:1–2). And because He is God incarnate, we can depend totally and absolutely on the trustworthiness of Him and His Word.

In this third Beatitude we have the words "(Happy) are the meek: for they shall inherit the earth." Has it ever occurred to you that there is happiness in meekness?

Searching for the Meaning of Meekness

To most people today the word "meek" brings to mind a picture of someone who is a weak personality, someone who allows everyone to walk over him. Meekness, in fact, in the popular mind is not seen as a desirable personality trait. Our society says, "Get ahead by intimidation" or "Look out for Number One." In the eyes of many people the only way to get ahead is to disregard other people and shove them out of the way. "I want to climb the ladder of success," one woman was quoted as saying, "and I don't care whose fingers I step on as I climb up the rungs."

But what does Jesus mean when He speaks of meekness? Does He, for example, mean that we are to be cringing before God, fearful of Him and slavishly yielding to His will because of fear of what He might do to us if we fail?

Could it be that Christ wanted His followers to be like the subdued puppy that comes crawling into its master's presence whipped and beaten? Is happiness the result of forced submission? Certainly not!

Jesus is not trying to convey the thought that God is an autocrat whose ego can be satisfied only by coerced yielding. Nothing could be further from the truth. There is no happiness in being compelled to do what you do not wish to do. No employees are more miserable than those who constantly resent their position in life. It would be against God's nature, as well as against man's free moral agency, to demand an allegiance which is not freely offered.

God conducts Himself in keeping with His righteousness. He will never violate our freedom to choose between eternal life and spiritual death, good and evil, right and wrong. His ultimate goal is not only to glorify Himself but also to make a happy relationship with His crowning creation—man. Never will He make any demands which encroach upon our freedom to choose.

Or does the meekness to which Jesus refers mean *weakness?* Does it mean that a special blessing is to be given to the feeble, the frail, or the fragile?

Certainly God has a special concern for those who are weak and powerless in this world. "Like as a father pitieth his children, so the Lord pitieth them that fear him. For he knoweth our frame; he remembereth that we are dust" (Psalm 103:13–14). But this is not what Jesus means by meekness here. The disciples were to be meek, but not weak and vacillating. They were to be disciplined, but not subdued and harmless in the face of evil.

Or does Jesus refer to those who are by nature mild-tempered? Some people are born with nicer dispositions than others. Their mild manner is not so much the product of prayer and spiritual grace as it is a matter of heredity. They are mild because their mother, or father or grandmother was mild-mannered. This is an admirable trait, but Jesus surely didn't refer to these fortunate few who by nature have good dispositions. That would mean that many who have dispositions like buzz saws could never know this happiness to which He refers.

In His characteristic way, Jesus was saying something quite shocking and quite revolutionary to His listeners in these words: "Happy are the meek." He was saying something quite the opposite to our modern concept of the way to happiness.

We say, "Happy are the clever, for these shall inherit the admiration of their friends"; "Happy are the aggressive for they shall inherit prosperity"; "Happy are the talented, for they shall inherit a career"; "Happy are the rich, for they shall inherit a world of friends and a house full of modern gadgets."

The True Meaning of Meekness

What, then, did Jesus mean? The dictionary says that the word *meek* means "mild, submissive, and compliant." William

Barclay points out that the Greek word for "meek" was the word which was often used to describe an animal which had been tamed to obey the command of its master. It might be a strong animal like a horse or ox, able to do a great deal of work. It was not "weak"— but it was "meek," always obedient to the will of its owner. A tame horse contributes much more to life than a wild one. Energy out of control is dangerous; energy under control is powerful.

That is a vivid picture of what Jesus means by "meekness." When we are apart from Christ we are, in a sense, like a wild animal. We live according to our own desires and wishes, obeying our own instincts and ruling our own lives. But when we come to Christ our goal is different. Now we want to live for Him and do His will. This, after all, is God's will for us, for Christ "died for all, that they which live should not henceforth live unto themselves, but unto him which died for them, and rose again" (2 Corinthians 5:15). We are "meek," submissive to the will of our Master and ready to work for Him. And when our lives and hearts are marked by true meekness, we will know true happiness.

Jesus did not say, "Be meek, and you shall inherit the earth." He, more than anyone else, knew that meekness was a gift of God, a result of a rebirth, a new life within.

Moses was meek, but he was not meek by nature. He slew an Egyptian in anger, and on more than one occasion he showed that he was not naturally meek. When he found the children of Israel turning from the Lord and worshiping idols, he became angry and dashed to the ground the tablets of stone upon which were inscribed the Ten Commandments. His meekness quite obviously was contrary to his nature. It was a miracle of God! Numbers 12:3 says, "Now the man Moses was very meek, above all the men which were upon the face of the earth."

Peter was not meek by nature. He became angry and cut off the ear of a guard who had come to arrest Jesus.(And I think we can safely assume he was aiming for his neck!) He swore profusely and angrily when accused of being one of Jesus' disciples. And yet he became one of the meekest of men and one of the strongest, most virile exponents of Christianity. Where did he get his meekness?

Paul, before his conversion, was not meek. Proudly and brutally he apprehended all Christians and sought to destroy them. He was bigoted, selfish, and boastful. But when he wrote his warm and affectionate letter to the churches of Galatia, he said, among other things: "The fruit of the Spirit is . . . gentleness, goodness . . . meekness" (Galatians 5:22, 23). His meekness was something God-given not something man-made.

It is not our human nature to be meek. On the contrary, it is our nature to be proud and haughty. That is why the new birth is so essential to each of us. That is why Jesus frankly and pointedly said not only to Nicodemus but to every one of us: "Ye must be born again" (John 3:7).

Meekness begins there! You must have a change of nature. Do you want this happiness? Then you must be born again—this is the first step! If you are too proud, stubborn, and willful to take this first step, then you do not qualify to inherit the earth.

When we reject this command of Christ, we automatically forfeit our right to His subsequent promises. We cannot end right when we begin wrong. If there is no rebirth, there can be no imparted meekness. And if there is no meekness, there can be no genuine happiness.

Arrogance has its own built-in misery. Arrogant people may offend others, but they hurt themselves more. My feelings of anger hurt me more than they do the people I'm angry at!

I was once stung by a honeybee. The sting hurt me, but it killed the bee. It died as a result of that thrust, but I didn't. In like manner, I may lash out at someone in anger. Yes, they may be hurt by my action—but like the bee I am the one who is hurt even more.

Muggings and vigilante attacks in retaliation, have become commonplace; and they are only the tip of the iceberg. Fathers and mothers wrangle and bicker. Abuse of children and the elderly is rampant. Homes are disintegrating. High government officials in Washington engage in name-calling and in heated disputes not at all in keeping with the dignity of their office.

Why and how has all this savagery crept into our social life? It is because we have forgotten Jesus' words: "Happy are the meek: for they shall inherit the earth."

We have glamorized vice and minimized virtue. We have played down gentleness, manners, and morals—while we have played up rudeness, savagery, and vice. We have reverted to the barbaric era of "tooth and claw," "the survival of the fittest," and the philosophy of "might is right." We are rich in knowledge but poor in wisdom; rich in the know-how of war but sadly lacking in gentleness, meekness, and faith. Individually, we are mechanisms of resentment, irritation, bitterness, and frustration!

Meekness Means Gentleness

The word *gentle* was rarely heard of before the Christian era and the word *gentleman* was not known. This high quality of character was a direct by-product of Christian faith.

The Bible says: "The wisdom that is from above is first pure, then peaceable, *gentle,* and easy to be intreated, full of mercy and good fruits, without partiality, and without hypocrisy" (James 3: 17).

St. Francis of Sales said: "Nothing is so strong as gentlemen; nothing so gentle as real strength." Charles Dickens wrote: "A man can never be a true gentleman in manner until he is a true gentleman at heart."

I have seen tough, rough, hardened men open their hearts by faith, receive Christ as Savior and become gentle, patient, merciful gentlemen.

I remember, when we were in London, the Ford Motor Company lent us two new Fords and employed two drivers to take our team to their various assignments. One of the chauffeurs was a typical roughneck who had missed little of what this world had to offer. He came to the meetings and looked on the scene perfunctorily with an occupational detachment. But one night he was moved to go to the counseling room and make his decision for Christ. You never saw such a change come over a man! His hardness disappeared; his veneer of sophistication melted away. He was a new creature! He threw away his X-rated literature, began to memorize the New Testament, and took on the true marks of a Christian gentleman. The fruit of the Spirit is ". . . gentleness, goodness . . . *meekness*" (Galatians 5:22, 23).

Of Eric Liddell, the missionary and great runner whose story is told in the film, "Chariots of Fire," someone has said, he was ". . . ridiculously humble in victory, utterly generous in defeat." That's a good definition of what it means to be meek.

Meekness Involves Yieldedness

The word *yield* has two meanings. The first is negative and the second is positive. It means "to relinquish, to abandon"; and also "to give." This is in line with Jesus' words: "He that loseth (or abandoneth) his life . . . shall find it" (Matthew 10:39).

We have heard the modern expression "Don't fight it—it's bigger than both of us." Those who are meek do not fight back at life. They learn the secret of surrender, of yielding to God. He then fights for us!

The Bible says: "For as ye have yielded your members servants to uncleanness and to iniquity . . . even so now yield your members servants to righteousness unto holiness" (Romans 6:19).

Instead of filling your mind with resentments, abusing your body by sinful diversion, and damaging your soul by willfulness, humbly give all over to God. Your conflicts will disappear and your inner tensions will vanish into thin air.

Then your life will begin to count for something. It will begin to yield, to produce, to bear fruit. You will have the feeling of belonging to life. Boredom will melt away and you will become vibrant with hope and expectation. Because you are meekly yielded, you will begin to "inherit the earth" of good things which God holds in store for those who trust Him with their all.

Even science teaches in unmistakable terms the Christian concept of entire surrender. Thomas Huxley once wrote Charles Kingsley: "Science says to sit down before the facts as a little child, be prepared to give up every preconceived notion, be willing to be led to whatever end Nature will lead you, or you will know nothing." S. I. McMillen said: "Surrendering one's will to the divine will may seem a negative procedure, but it gives positive dividends."

Happy are the meek. Happy are the yielded. Happy are those who trustingly put their lives, their fortunes, and their future in the capable hands of their Creator. Happy are those who "let go and let God."

God does not discipline us to subdue us, but to condition us for a life of usefulness and blessedness. In His wisdom He knows that an uncontrolled life is an unhappy life, so He puts reins upon our wayward souls that they may be directed into the "paths of righteousness." That is what God seeks to do with us: to tame us, to bring us under proper control so we can do His will.

"I beseech you therefore, brethren, by the mercies of God, that ye present your bodies a living sacrifice, holy, acceptable unto God, which is your reasonable service. And be not conformed to this world: but be ye transformed by the renewing of your mind, that ye may prove what is that good, and acceptable, and perfect, will of God" (Romans 12:1–2).

God does in the spiritual realm what science does in the physical realm. Science takes a Niagara River with its violent turbulence and transforms it into electrical energy to illuminate a million homes and to turn the productive wheels of industry.

God took Peter—a zealot, a political reactionary of his day—and diverted his energy and his unbounding enthusiasm to high purposes instead of low, and he helped lead a movement which reshaped the world.

He took Matthew—a suave, tricky politician, who knew the political ropes well enough to keep from dangling from one of them by the neck—and, putting the bridle of grace upon him, changed him into an agent of blessing.

God had to do a job of taming with each of the disciples. Taming was not a matter of doing away with their powers and their energies but of *redirecting* them.

You have a *temper!* There is nothing unique about that. Most people have tempers, in varying degrees of course. God does not ask that you get rid of that temper. But He does say that if you are to be happy, it must be brought under control and rechanneled to proper use. God does not use a person without a temper as well as He does one with a controlled temper. There are too many professed Christians who never get "wrought up" about anything; they never get indignant with injustice, with corruption in high places, or with the godless traffics which barter away the souls and bodies of people. Someone has said, "There are some things that don't improve the longer you keep them. There are others that do. Your temper is one of them." The Bible warns about an uncontrolled temper, "A wrathful man stirreth up strife: but he that is slow to anger appeaseth strife" (Proverbs 15:18).

You have an *ego*—a consciousness of being an individual! Of course you do, and God does not ask you to get rid of that ego. In fact, it is important for us to have a right understanding of our value and importance—what the psychologists call a healthy self-image. But we develop that best when we begin to see ourselves as God sees us—as persons who are so valuable to Him that He wants us to be forgiven and cleansed of sin so we can be His children. But that doesn't mean that you are to worship yourself, to think constantly of yourself, and to live entirely for self. Common sense tells you that your life would be miserable if you followed that course. God is infinitely more concerned about your happiness than you could possibly be. He says, "Deny yourself, and follow Me."

There are people in our mental institutions today who thought excessively about themselves, to the exclusion of God and others. Hypochondriacs who have a fanciful anxiety about their health will never be well regardless of their physical condition. They remind me of the people who have this sign on their desk: "*I* am planning to have a nervous breakdown. *I* have earned it. *I* deserve it. *I* worked for it and nobody is going to keep me from having it!"

Each of us has a *tongue* and a *voice*. These instruments of speech can be used destructively or employed constructively.

I can use my tongue to slander, to gripe, to scold, to nag, and to quarrel; or I can bring it under the control of God's Spirit and make it an instrument of blessing and praise. The Bible says, "The tongue is a little member, and boasteth great things. Behold, how great a matter a little fire kindleth! And the tongue is a fire, a world of iniquity" (James 3:5–6). Only God can control it, as we yield it to Him.

The twentieth-century version of James 3:3 says, "When we put bits into the horses' mouths to make them obey us, we control the rest of their bodies also." Just so, when we submit to the claims of Christ upon our lives, our untamed natures are brought under His control. We become meek, tamed, and "fit for the Master's service."

Meekness Denotes Forbearance

"Forbearance" is a word which has been almost dropped from our modern vocabulary. It means to abstain from condemning others, to refrain from judging the actions and motives of those about us.

The Bible says: "With all lowliness and meekness, with long-suffering, forbearing one another in love" (Ephesians 4:2).

This generation is quick with the deadly thrust but slow with the ointment of healing. The harsh criticism of others and unfair appraisals of those about us may hurt them, but it hurts us more. The unjust condemnation of others has a boomerang effect. I hurl my vindictive indictments with the hope of crippling others, but, alas, I discover that I am hurt more than they are.

Many a person is lonely today because he has driven away by his own bitterness and harsh words the very friends he needed. Many a wife has discovered that scolding and nagging will never win a husband but often results in a divorce situation.

Some people go through their entire lives with a "chip on their shoulder," carrying hurts and resentments over things that were said or done decades ago. Like a poison, their bitterness has made not only their own lives miserable but the lives of those around them. They have never learned the secret of forgiveness and forbearance. The Bible warns us to be on guard "lest any root of bitterness springing up trouble you, and thereby many be defiled" (Hebrews 12:15).

Meekness and forbearance are "musts" if I am to live harmoniously in society and if I want to build a happy family life.

The Bible says: "Speak evil of no man . . . but (be) gentle, showing all meekness unto all men" (Titus 3:2). I cannot be happy as long as I magnify the faults of others and minimize their virtues. This is a good way to frighten away my friends, forfeit my domestic happiness, and fritter away a rosy future.

Here is the Christian answer to neighborhood quarrels, to family fusses, and community feuds: "Forbearing one another, and forgiving one another, if any man have a quarrel against any: even as Christ forgave you, so also do ye" (Colossians 3:13).

There is a story told of a devout old deacon who, goaded apparently beyond endurance by the persistent malice of an enemy, publicly vowed to "kill him." His enemy heard of his intentions and waited sardonically to see what the harmless old saint would do. Actually, instead of rendering evil for evil, the old deacon sought out every opportunity to do his enemy good. This was at first a source of merriment and some slight annoyance, but when at last the deacon rendered an unquestioned sacrificial service to his enemy by risking his life to save the man's wife from drowning, the deadlock between them was broken.

"All right," said his enemy, "you've done what you said you would do. You've killed me—or at least you've killed the man I was. Now, what can I do for you?"

This world is not yet impervious to a solid Christian act! What the world needs is not more Christianity but more Christians who practice Christian forbearance and forgiveness.

Meekness Suggests Patience

This is a high-strung, neurotic, impatient age. We hurry when there is no reason to hurry, just to be hurrying. This fast-paced age has produced more problems and less morality than previous generations, and it has given all of us a set of jangled nerves. Thomas à Kempis said: "All men commend patience, although few be willing to practice it." John F. Newton wrote: "Be patient enough to live one day at a time as Jesus taught us, letting yesterday go, and leaving tomorrow till it arrives."

Impatience has produced a new crop of broken homes, a million or more new ulcers, and has set the stage for more world wars. In no area of our lives has it been more damaging than on the domestic scene. This homely little couplet bespeaks the rack and ruin modern life has wrought in our homes:

> Theirs was a "beef stew" marriage,
> And their case was somewhat crude—
> The wife was always "beefing,"
> And the husband, always "stewed."

But the Bible says: "But let patience have her perfect work, that ye may be perfect and entire, wanting nothing" (James 1:4).

I know of a woman—a professed Christian—who, though good in many respects, was very impatient. Her pastor one day spoke to her husband about his soul, and the man replied, "My wife is a good homemaker, but if religion would make me as impatient as she is, I want no part of it."

The minister had a frank talk with the woman, and in tears and humility she confessed that her sin was the sin of impatience. A few days later her husband came in from fishing. As he walked through the living room with rod in hand, he accidentally knocked over a prized vase that went crashing to the floor. His wife ran into the room, and he braced himself for the second crash—a tirade of words from his nervous wife. But instead, she smilingly said, "Think nothing of it, dear, accidents happen in the best of families."

We will not pursue the story any further except to say that a few weeks later he made his decision for Christ and became a staunch worker in the church. He saw Christianity in practice in the life of his wife!

The apostle Peter declared that some husbands "though they do not obey the word, may be won without a word by the behavior of their wives, when they see your reverent and chaste behavior. . . . with the imperishable jewel of a gentle and quiet spirit, which in God's sight is very precious" (1 Peter 3:1–2, RSV).

The world believes that Christianity is a good thing, but Christians have too often failed to "adorn the doctrine" by living meek and patient lives.

"Happy are the meek: for they shall inherit the earth." Only those who are contrite, humble, and submissively dependent upon God can inherit the earth of radiance, joy, and contentment.

Jesus said to Saul: "It is hard for thee to kick against the pricks" (Acts 9:5; 26:14). The pricks He referred to were goads which were in the harness of the oxen to keep them under control. They were not put there to harm the ox but to make him useful, to direct his energies constructively.

Many of you reading these words have been "kicking against the pricks." Your quarrel has not been so much with others, as you thought, as it has been with yourself. God does not want you to live in constant rebellion against life, its seeming injustices, its hurts and its wrongs. He bids you to stop your futile strivings, to surrender your resentments, to yield your will, and to exercise gentleness and patience. Then you will be happy, and others about you will see Christ in you and will be drawn toward Him.

Meekness is not something I can acquire by myself. It is not something I can get in college or in a scientific laboratory. It is not something I inherit. It is God-given! Jesus said: "Take my yoke upon you, and learn of me; for I am meek and lowly in heart: and ye shall find rest unto your souls" (Matthew 11:29).

Happiness and Meekness for You

Go into a television store and notice all the televisions on display. On some of them bright pictures are to be seen, filled with vibrant colors and giving out the sounds of the latest program. But there are others on display which are only sitting there, their screens dark and silent. Your eye naturally goes to the sets that are on; there is nothing particularly interesting about a dark television screen. What is the difference? Only one thing: the dark television sets are not connected to the power. And that can be true of us, if we try to develop true meekness apart from God. We need to have a living relationship with Him.

God is no respecter of persons. Each of us deserves our just share of happiness. Each of us has the same capacity for God. I should not stand back lamenting my bad luck and my bad breaks in life. I should be joined to the source of power. Take Christ's yoke upon you, "and ye shall find rest unto your soul."

"But I can't live it! I would surely fail in the attempt to be a Christian!" you protest.

Jesus said: "Take my yoke upon you." It is His yoke, and

77

I may rest assured that He will bear the heavy part of the load.

Before He left His disciples, Christ promised that He would send a Comforter to help them in the trials, cares, and temptations of life. This word *comforter* means "one that helps alongside." He is the Holy Spirit, the powerful Third Person of the Trinity. The moment we are born again He takes up residence in our hearts.

We may not emotionally feel Him there, but here again we must exercise faith. Believe it! Accept it as a fact of faith! He is in our hearts to help us to be meek!

We are told that He sheds the love of God abroad in our hearts. He produces the fruit of the Spirit: "love, joy, peace, longsuffering, gentleness, goodness, faith, meekness, temperance" (Galatians 5:22–23). We cannot possibly manufacture this fruit in our own cannery. It is supernaturally manufactured by the Holy Spirit who lives in our hearts!

I must yield to Him . . . surrender to Him . . . give Him control of my life. Then through the meekness I receive from Him I will find happiness!

*Blessed are they which do hunger and
thirst after righteousness: for they shall
be filled.* Matthew 5:6

CHAPTER FIVE

Happy though Hungry

"Two verbs have built two empires," wrote St. Augustine, "the verb *to have* and the verb *to be*. The first is an empire of things, material possessions and power. The second is an empire of the Spirit, things that last."

This fourth Beatitude of Christ expresses a crucial, central truth. When Jesus spoke these words: "Happy are they which do hunger and thirst after righteousness," He addressed them to the multitude. It was not enough to be hungry and thirsty. The important question was, "What were they hungry *for*?"

The multitude on that torrid, sultry day in Palestine symbolizes the great parade of men and women down through the centuries. What He said to them, He says to us and has been saying to all people through the years. Most of the people in that throng were deprived spiritually, socially, and economically. Their hungers were very deep, but none would be more important than their spiritual longings and yearnings. How "righteous" is our society at its core? Perhaps a couple of stories from the daily news will help to answer this question.

A Sick Society

Even the interns at San Francisco General Hospital flinched when they saw the injuries of a young policeman who was carried in on a stretcher. His cheek was bloody from an ugly wound, he was in agony from a savage kick in the groin, and his nose was broken after being stomped on by a teenager's foot. Forty minutes earlier he had tried to arrest two drunken rowdies on Market Street in the heart of downtown San Francisco. A crowd had gathered almost at once.

"The people stood around gawking and laughing at me," the officer said. "When other hoodlums tried to take away my prisoners, numbers of the crowd held my arms. One took my gun, and they let the thugs beat me. Some even joined in the assault. Nobody tried to help me."

More mystified than critical, the officer stared up at the hospital ceiling and asked wonderingly, "What's happened to the people these days? Many of them act as if policemen are their enemies."

This injured officer was the victim of a social malady which is threatening the peace of this nation. There is a growing contempt for authority and for law.

In Los Angeles, two officers arrested two boys who were

creating a disturbance in an amusement park. Quickly the police were surrounded by a cursing, jeering mob of several hundred people. Bricks were hurled, bats and jack handles were wielded, and the police cars were overturned.

The attitude toward officers is so menacing in New York City that the Police Commissioner has ordered a special tactical patrol force to disperse the taunting, dangerous mobs which try to interfere with the work of the police. The hazards of police work are increasing. In New York City alone, nearly fifteen hundred policemen were attacked by bystanders, youths, and passersby, in one recent eight-month period. The Commissioner of Police in New York City says grimly, "The police cannot fight crime and the public at the same time."

There are many contributing causes to the rioting and crime wave in the nation. Certainly one of the contributing elements is poverty. But another contributing element is found in the home.

Much of today's disrespect for authority stems from a disorganized or indifferent family life. Young people reflect the attitudes of their parents. Even though the overwhelming majority of Americans want law, order, peace, and security, an increasingly vocal minority is revolutionary in its attitude. Until the attitude of government, the family, the home, the church, the courts becomes predominantly righteous, our democratic form of government is in danger of being overthrown. What is the answer to our problem?

We can give people social and economic freedom, but if their thirst for fellowship with God remains unquenched, they will still behave like animals. Witness the prosperity of Western civilization at this very moment. We have everything a machine age can provide, yet boredom and unhappiness have reached an all-time high and our morals have plunged to an all-time low. The reason: our hunger for God has not been dulled or wiped out by other things. We have dulled our hunger and quenched our thirst with the desire for money, security, fame, and success.

A man and his wife visited an orphanage where they hoped to adopt a child. In an interview with the boy they wanted, they told him in glowing terms about the many things they could give him. To their amazement, the little fellow said, "If you have nothing to offer except a good home, clothes, toys, and the other things that most kids have—why—I would just as soon stay here."

"What on earth could you want besides those things?" the woman asked.

"I just want someone to love me," replied the little boy.

There you have it! Even a little boy knows that "man shall not live by bread alone" (Matthew 4:4; Luke 4:4).

The heart cannot be satisfied with computers and sophisticated video equipment. We were created "a little lower than the angels" (Hebrews 2:7) and our souls can never subsist on the husks of this pleasure-seeking world. Our deeper yearnings and longings can be met only by a renewed fellowship with the One in whose image we were created: God. As St. Augustine said, "Thou hast made us for Thyself and our hearts are restless till they find their rest in Thee."

Happiness in Hunger

"Happy are they which do hunger and thirst after righteousness: for they shall be filled."

We can all understand the metaphor which Jesus employed here—hunger. We have all experienced some time in our lives the gnawing pain, the dizziness, and the faint feeling which accompanies intense hunger. We know what it is to experience the dry parchedness of thirst. We have also seen the haunting pictures on television of painfully thin mothers bending over little children with swollen bellies and vacant eyes, tragic victims of famine in Africa or other parts of the world. So, quite naturally, we come to attention when He says: "Happy are they which do hunger and thirst."

But what happiness is there in hunger and thirst?

Well, to begin with, hunger is a sign of life. Dead men need no food, they crave no water.

The Bible teaches that it is possible through lack of spiritual earnestness to harden one's heart as Pharaoh did long ago. This is one of the most dangerous processes that can take place in the human soul. It is possible through sin to harden our hearts against God so long that we lose all desire for God. Then the Scripture says: "God gave them up" (Psalm 81:12; Romans 1:24).

If I have the slightest bit of hunger in my heart for God and righteousness, then it is a certain sign that it is not too hardened to be receptive to the voice and message of Christ. I am yet alive and sensitive to the Spirit's voice.

Those who have no cravings for God, no longings for

Christ, and no thirst for the things of the Spirit are not only dead in trespasses and sins, but they are also insensitive to the Spirit's promptings. They are like the dead and are in danger of remaining in a state of spiritual stupor that will lead eventually to eternal death.

A man once told me that he nearly froze to death in the far north. His hands lost their feeling, his feet became numb, and he was overcome with an impulse to lie down in the snow and go to sleep when it dawned upon him that he was freezing to death. He jumped up and ran vigorously until his circulation was stimulated. If he had not suddenly become conscious that he was dying and acted upon that consciousness, he would have frozen to death.

Happy are those who respond to the Spirit's warnings. They alone have hope of being filled.

A hungry person is a normal person. Those who are sick and abnormally upset refuse nourishment, but the normal person craves food. In that sense there is a blessedness in hunger. It is a natural reaction.

The normal person also possesses a spiritual hunger—although he may not label it as such. He may think he has filled it, but apart from God there is no lasting quenching of his spiritual hunger and thirst. David said: "As the hart panteth after the water brooks, so panteth my soul after thee, O God" (Psalm 42:1).

Isaiah said: "With my soul have I desired thee in the night; yea, with my spirit within me will I seek thee early: for when thy judgments are in the earth, the inhabitants of the world will learn righteousness" (Isaiah 26:9).

Each of us was created in the image and likeness of God. We were made for God's fellowship, and our hearts can never be satisfied without His communion. Just as iron is attracted to a magnet, the soul in its state of hunger is drawn to God. Though you, like thousands of others may feel in the state of sin that the world is more alluring and more to your liking, someday—perhaps even now as you read these words—you will acknowledge that there is something deep down inside you which cannot be satisfied by the alloy of earth.

Then with David, the Psalmist (who had sampled the delicacies of sin and had found them unsatisfying), you will say: "O God, thou art my God; early will I seek thee: my soul thirsteth for thee, my flesh longeth for thee in a dry and thirsty land, where no water is" (Psalm 63:1).

The trouble with most of us is that we make happiness our goal instead of aiming at something higher, loftier, and nobler. Unhappiness is like pain—it is only an effect of an underlying cause. Pain cannot be relieved until the cause is removed. Pain and disease go together: disease is the cause, and pain is the effect.

Unhappiness is an effect, and sin is the cause. Sin and unhappiness go together. All was blissful happiness in the Garden of Eden until sin crept in. Then happiness crept out. The two just cannot exist together.

Hunger for Righteousness

What is this righteousness we are to desire? Is this righteousness to which Jesus referred in the fourth Beatitude a religious experience? Is it some mysterious ecstasy which comes to only a few people fraught with cataclysmic emotions and spiritual sensations?

Any kind of religious experience which does not produce righteousness in our lives is a counterfeit and not worth seeking. Today there are all kinds of cults and philosophies which claim to have the power to change our lives for the better—but they cannot live up to their claim because they have no power to change the human heart. At worst, they end up enslaving their adherents. But God's will is that we would be righteous in our living. God is holy, and the whole scheme of redemption has holiness for its goal. The apostle Peter declared that Christ was the one "Who his own self bare our sins in his own body on the tree, that we, being dead to sins, should live unto righteousness" (1 Peter 2:24).

The kind of religious experience which does not produce righteousness in the life is hardly worth seeking. But religious demonstrations that do not create in us better morals and a Christlikeness of character serve no useful purpose and could certainly do more harm than good. God is holy, and the whole scheme of redemption has holiness for its goal.

Nor is this righteousness to which Jesus referred a perfunctory, mechanical performance of religious rites. Jesus taught the futility of holding to religious theory apart from Christian practice when He said: "Except your righteousness shall exceed the righteousness of the scribes and Pharisees, ye shall in no case enter into the kingdom of heaven" (Matthew 5:20).

Neither is righteousness an abstract, speculative morality

86

so prevalent in the world today. Many people condemn sin in high places but fail to recognize it in their own personal lives. They condemn it in the government and society but condone it in their own hearts.

It is just as sinful in God's sight for an individual to break the marriage vow as it is for a nation to break a treaty.

The Nature of Righteousness

What is this righteousness that Jesus exhorts us to hunger for? The Bible teaches that God is holy, righteous, and pure. He cannot tolerate sin in His presence. However, man has chosen to disregard the divine laws and standards. As a result of man's transgressions, he is called a "sinner." Sin immediately breaks his fellowship with God. Man becomes unrighteous, impure, and unholy in the sight of God. A holy God cannot have fellowship with that which is unholy, unrighteous, and unethical. Therefore, sin breaks off friendship with God. Man is called in the Bible an "alien," an "enemy" to God, and a "sinner" against Him. The only way that man can again have fellowship with God and find the happiness that he longs for is to find some way to possess a righteousness and holiness that will commend him to God.

Many have tried to reform to gain favor with God. Some have mutilated their bodies and tortured themselves, thinking thereby to gain favor with God. Others have thought that if they would work hard and live moral lives, they could somehow justify themselves.

But the Bible teaches that all our righteousness—falling

short of the divine standard as it does—is as filthy rags in the sight of God. There is absolutely no possibility of our manufacturing a righteousness, holiness, or goodness that will satisfy God. Even the best of us is impure to God.

I remember what happened one day many years ago when my wife was doing the washing. This was before we had a clothes dryer. The clothes looked white and clean in the house, but when she hung them on the line they actually appeared soiled and dirty in contrast to the fresh-fallen snow.

Our own lives may seem at times to be morally good and decent; but, in comparison to the holiness and the purity of God, we are defiled and filthy.

In spite of our sins and moral uncleanness, God loves us. He decided to provide a righteousness for us. This is the reason that He gave His Son, Jesus Christ, to die on the cross.

Have you ever stopped to think why it is the cross has become the symbol of Christianity? It is because at the cross Jesus purchased our redemption and provided a righteousness which we could not ourselves earn. "The gift of God is eternal life through Jesus Christ our Lord" (Romans 6:23). On the ground of faith in the atoning death and resurrection of His Son, God has provided and ascribed righteousness for all who will receive it.

This means that God forgives all past sin and failure. He wipes the slate clean. He takes our sins and buries them in the depths of the sea and removes them as far as the east is from the west.

To use another illustration from the Bible, in our natural state we are clothed with filthy rags because of our sin, and we cannot come into the presence of God our King. But God in Christ takes away our old filthy garments and clothes us instead with new garments—the pure white garments of Christ! As the old hymn declares:

> When He shall come with trumpet sound,
> Oh, may I then in Him be found;
> Dressed in His righteousness alone,
> Faultless to stand before the throne.

Our God Forgets!

The omniscient God has the unique ability that we do not have: He has the ability to forget. The God of grace forgets our sins and wipes them completely from His memory forever! He places us in His sight as though we had never committed one sin.

In theological language, this is called *justification*. The Bible says: "Therefore being justified by faith, we have peace with God through our Lord Jesus Christ" (Romans 5:1).

There is no possibility of true happiness until we have established friendship and fellowship with God. And there is no possibility of establishing this fellowship apart from the cross of His Son, Jesus Christ. God says, "I will forgive you, but I will forgive you only at the foot of the cross." He says, "I will fellowship with you, but I will fellowship with you only at the cross." That is the reason it is necessary for us to come to the cross in repentance of our sin and by faith in His Son to find forgiveness and salvation.

The Goal of Righteousness

As we have noted, when we come to Christ God imparts His righteousness to us. It is almost as if an accounting entry had been made in the books of Heaven, declaring us righteous for Christ's sake!

But when we come to Christ by faith and receive Him as our Savior our "hunger and thirst after righteousness" are not ended. Yes, my sins have been washed away and my salvation is secure in Christ. But I also know that within my soul there still is sin. My motives are not pure; my tongue may not be tamed; my love for others may be dim. It is God's will for this to be changed, however, and for us to exhibit increasingly in our lives the righteousness of Christ. "Let your light so shine before men, that they may see your good works, and glorify your father which is in heaven" (Matthew 5:16).

Sometimes I have had persons who have not been Christians very long come to me and say that they had decided they must never have been Christians after all. When I have asked them why, they have replied that everything seemed fine for a few weeks after their decision for Christ, but then they found themselves committing sin. They had thought—mistakenly—that if they were Christ's they would never sin again. But that is not true! As long as we are in the flesh we will always be engaged in a continual battle against sin in our lives.

But it is not God's will for us to continue in sin—and in fact, if we are completely indifferent to the presence of sin in our lives the Bible indicates we do not really know Christ. Instead, we are to "hunger and thirst after righteousness"—to pursue righteousness and purity with God's help, so that our lives become increasingly like Christ every day.

Righteousness is something which we do not possess as a natural gift, but it is a God-given gift to be specially received. It is a bit of heaven brought to earth. The righteousness of the God-man is applied to us in justification and in sanctification, so that righteousness is progressively implanted in the believer's heart. It is God's sharing His nature with us. We become partakers of divine life.

Now, God says that only those who hunger after it will receive it. God thrusts this heavenly manna on no one.

We must desire it, above everything else. Our yearning for God must supersede all other desires. It must be like a gnawing hunger and a burning thirst.

There are several things that can spoil our appetite for the righteousness of God.

Stumbling Blocks to Righteousness

FIRST: *Sinful pleasure* can ruin our appetite for the things of God.

Paul had a young co-laborer in the gospel named Demas. Because his appetite for the pleasures of the world was greater than his thirst for God, we hear very little of young Demas. Paul wrote his entire history in nine words: "Demas hath forsaken me, having loved this present world" (2 Timothy 4:10).

Many of us have no appetite for spiritual things because we are absorbed in the sinful pleasures of this world. We have been eating too many of the devil's delicacies.

I once heard the story of a man walking down the road to market. A pig followed behind him. All the other farmers were driving their pigs, struggling to get them to market. A friend called to him and asked him how he got the pig to follow him. He said, "It's very simple. Every step I take, I drop a bean, and the pig likes beans."

Satan goes along the road of life dropping his beans, and we are following him to eternal destruction.

Our sins may be very obvious and open, or they may be very respectable or subtle. Perhaps we are preoccupied with material things which, while not wrong in themselves, have wrapped their tentacles around us and are squeezing out our spiritual hunger and thirst for righteousness. We may be preoccupied with our career or our education, or any of hundreds of other things which can dull our appetite for God and His righteousness.

SECOND: *Self-sufficiency* can impair our hunger after God. No one is so empty as he who thinks he is full. No one is so ill as he who has a fatal disease and yet thinks he is in perfect health. No one is so poor as he who thinks he is rich but is actually bankrupt.

The Bible says: "Thou sayest, I am rich, and increased with goods, and have need of nothing; and knowest not that thou art wretched, and miserable, and poor, and blind, and naked" (Revelation 3:17).

A person who is filled with himself has no room for God in his life. Self-sufficiency can ruin one's appetite for the things of Christ.

THIRD: *Secret sin* can take away our appetite for the righteousness of God.

That secret sin we commit has a price. We may think we've kept our sin a secret, but remorse for it will remain in our hearts. Those evil resentments we harbor in our minds against our neighbor! The failure to forgive those who have wronged us! When the heart is filled with wickedness, there is no room for God. The jealousies, the envies, the prejudices, and the malices will take away our appetite for the things of the Spirit.

Judas was one of the twelve disciples, outwardly a diligent follower of Christ. But in his heart he tolerated greed and evil and they led him to betray Jesus and eventually commit suicide. King Saul outwardly welcomed the young lad David into his palace, but in his heart he was filled with bitterness and jealousy of him. Eventually those secret sins consumed him and destroyed him.

When our lives are filled with the husks of prejudice and the chaff of resentment, we can have no thirst for righteousness. If we allow our hearts to be filled with Satan's rations, we will have no desire for heaven's manna.

FOURTH: *Neglect of our spiritual life* can take away our appetite for the righteousness of God.

All Christians believe in God, but nominal Christians have little time for God. They are too busy with everyday affairs to be concerned with Bible reading, prayer, and being thoughtful to their fellow men. Many have lost the spirit of a zealous discipleship.

If you ask them if they are Christians, they would probably answer, "I think so," or "I hope so." They may go to church at Easter and Christmas and other special occasions, but otherwise they have little time for God. They have crowded God out of their lives.

The Bible warns us against neglect of our souls. It is possible to harden our hearts and shrivel our souls until we lose our appetite for the things of God. Just like someone who refuses to eat and eventually grows weaker and weaker until he dies, so a person who is "too busy" for God will starve himself and wither away spiritually.

This hunger, then, that we should have is a desire to be always right with God. It is a consciousness that all searching for peace of heart except in Him is in vain. It is an admission of our own futility, our own helplessness, and our complete abandonment to His will.

Like Peter, who stepped out upon the waves of self-sufficiency only to find that they would not bear him up, we cry, "Master, save me, or I perish!"

Like the prodigal son, who sampled the devil's delicacies in the far-off city, we discover that the world's husks fill but do not satisfy. It is then in the knowledge of our real need that we say, "Father, I have sinned against heaven, and before thee. . . . make me as one of thy hired servants" (Luke 15:18, 19).

The prodigal son's "comeback" began down in the swine pen when he said, "How many hired servants of my father's have bread enough and to spare, and I perish with hunger!" (Luke 15:17). The very moment that he began to hunger, God began to "set the table" for spiritual reunion. His deepest yearnings and longings were not for food but for being reconciled to his father. The first thing he said was, "Father, I have sinned against heaven, and before thee, and am no more worthy to be called thy son. . . ."

Neither is our goal to be blessings, experiences, or even answers to our prayers, taken by themselves. These are all the accompaniment of being right with our Heavenly Father.

God, like the prodigal's father, says to all of those who hunger and thirst after righteousness, "Son, all that I have is yours."

But the key to spiritual satisfaction is being right with God. When through faith we are in the position of sonship, then God's riches become our riches; God's abundance, our abundance; God's power, our power. When a proper relationship has been restored between us and God, then happiness, contentment, and peace of mind will be a natural outgrowth of that restored relationship.

The Difference Between Believing and Receiving

You ask, "How can I start? What do I have to do?"

Jesus said: "You must be converted." The word *conversion* means to "turn around," to "change your mind," to "turn back," and to "return."

In many ways conversion is a mystery, for from our viewpoint as humans it is both man's work and God's work. Our responsibility is to turn to Christ in faith and repentance, turning from our sins and asking Him to come into our hearts by faith. We express our desire to change the course of our lives, and we acknowledge our helplessness to do this apart from God's help. We commit ourselves to live in accordance with God's will. And when we do, God the Holy Spirit comes to dwell within us. If our commitment is genuine, God works

in our hearts to regenerate us. Then we have truly been converted—we have been born again by the Spirit of God!

But many people immediately argue, "I do believe in
Christ. I believe in the Church, and I believe in the Bible.
Isn't that enough?"

No! We must *receive* Christ.

I may go to the airport. I have a reservation. I have a ticket
in my pocket. The plane is on the ramp. It is a big, powerful
plane. I am certain that it will take me to my destination.
They call the flight three times. I neglect to get on board.
They close the door. The plane taxis down the runway and
takes off. I am not on the plane. Why? I "believed" in the
plane, but I neglected to get on board.

That's just it! A person may believe in God, Christ, the
Bible, and the Church—but neglect to actually receive Him
in the heart. That kind of belief is impersonal and speculative. It does not involve complete *commitment* to Him.

The moment we receive Him, the Bible says, we are born
again. God's nature enters into our own souls, and we become a child of God in full spiritual fellowship.

This is what we might call the "vertical relationship," the
perpendicular companionship between God and man. It is
absolutely the first step toward happiness. There is no use
reading the rest of this book until you are absolutely sure
that you have repented of sin, received Christ by faith, and
been born again. The vertical relationship must always pre-
cede the "horizontal."

Our sustenance, our supply, our power come from above.
Man is like a tram or a streetcar. He must be connected ver-

tically (above) before he can move horizontally. Our relationship must be right with God before it can be right with man. And if this be true, then the converse is equally true—if we are wrong with God, we are wrong with man also.

There is a law in musical tone which says, "Two instruments tuned to the same pitch are in tune with each other." A similar rule in mathematics is: "Two quantities equal to the same quantity are equal to each other."

So two people in tune with God are in tune with each other. Two people in love with Christ have love for each other.

The moment I receive Christ as my Lord and Savior, Christ, through the Holy Spirit, comes to live in my heart. The Scripture says: "Christ in you, the hope of glory" (Colossians 1:27). We may not see Him with the natural eye and we may not feel Him with our emotions, but He is there nevertheless. We are to accept Him by faith!

This aspect of righteousness for which we are to hunger is called, in theological language, *sanctification*. Don't let this word frighten you. It actually means "separated" or "clean." In one sense, sanctification is instantaneous. The moment I receive Christ as Savior, the Holy Spirit comes into my heart.

There is also a sense in which sanctification is progressive. I grow in the grace and knowledge of Jesus Christ. Being a Christian is more than just an instantaneous conversion—it is a daily process whereby I grow to be more and more like Christ. When we start out, we begin as a baby does in physical life. We must be fed on the simple things of the Bible, and we learn to walk in our Christian life gradually. In Elizabeth Goudge's delightful book, *The Dean's Watch,* she describes a part of the saintly Miss Montague's spiritual pilgrimage: "Until now she had only read her Bible as a pious exercise, but now she read it as an engineer reads a blueprint and a traveler a map, unemotionally because she was not emotional, but with profound concentration because her life depended on it. Bit by bit over a period of years, that seemed to her long, she began to get her scaffolding in place." At first we fall down and make many mistakes, but we are to continue growing.

The Dangers of Spiritual Staleness

However, there are many people who have stopped growing. They remain spiritual babes all their lives. I am afraid that this experience is all too common today. Perhaps it is yours.

Do you remember the day when you gave your heart and your life to Christ? You were sure of victory. How easy it seemed to be more than conqueror through Christ who loved you. Under the leadership of a Captain who had never been foiled in battle, how could you dream of defeat?

And yet to many of you, how different has been your real experience! Your victories have been few and fleeting and your defeats many and disastrous. You have not lived as you feel children of God ought to live.

As Mrs. Hannah Whitall-Smith reminds us in her book *The Christian's Secret of a Happy Life*, "You have had, perhaps, a clear understanding of doctrinal truths but you have not come into possession of their light and power. In your life

Christ is believed in, talked about, and served, but He is not filling you hour by hour. You found Christ as your Savior from the penalty of sin, but you have not found Him as your all-sufficient Savior from its power. The joy and thrill of Christian experience is gone."

There is only a dying ember of what used to be a mighty prairie fire for Christ in your soul. In the very depths of your heart you know that your experience is not the scriptural experience. Down through the years it seems that all you can expect from your Christianity is a life of ultimate failure and defeat—one hour failure, and the next hour repenting and beginning again, only to fail again.

Vigor in the Early Church

We read in the Scriptures that the early church was filled with the Holy Spirit. They had no church buildings, no Bibles, no automobiles, no planes, no trains, no television, no radio. Yet they turned their world "upside down" for Christ. They instituted a spiritual revolution that shook the very foundations of the Roman Empire. They were young, vigorous, virile, powerful. They lived their lives daily for Christ. They suffered persecution and even death gladly for their faith in Christ. What was the secret of their success—even in the face of opposition and death? One reason beyond doubt is that they hungered and thirsted after righteousness. And those with whom they came in contact could not help but be impressed by the quality and purity of their lives and their love.

The reason certain false philosophies and religions are

making such inroads in the world today is that somewhere along the line the people who were supposed to live Christian lives failed. We have failed to meet the standards and requirements that Jesus set forth. If we would live for Christ we must be willing to count all else as "nothing but refuse." We must be as dedicated, as committed, and as willing to sacrifice all, as the followers of false religions are.

The great masses of the unbelieving world are confused as they gaze upon the strife within and among religious bodies. Instead of a dynamic, growing, powerful, Christ-centered Church, we see division, strife, pettiness, greed, jealousy, and spiritual laziness—while the world is standing on the brink of disaster.

The great need in Christendom today is for Christians to learn the secret of daily, wholehearted recommitment to Christ.

Paul himself spoke of his struggle. He spoke of desiring to please God, but in himself he found no strength to do so. The things he did not want to do he sometimes did; and the things he wanted to do he did not do. Nearly driven to distraction, Paul shouts out: "Who shall deliver me from the body of this death?" (Romans 7:24).

And in the next verse he records the answer to that all-important, searching, bewildering question when he says: "I thank God through Jesus Christ our Lord" (Romans 7:25).

Christ can be our Deliverer!

Many of us ask the questions: "Why do I, as a Christian, do some of the things I do? Why do I, as a Christian, leave undone the things I ought to have done?"

Many name the Name of Christ, but live in constant defeat. They have unclean hands, unclean lips, unclean tongues, unclean feet, unclean thoughts, unclean hearts—and yet claim to be Christians. They claim Christ, attend church, try to pray—and yet they know there are things in their souls that are not right. There is no joy in their hearts, no love for others. In fact, there is little evidence of the fruit of the Spirit in their lives. The fire in their souls has been quenched.

Yet as we look around, we do know some people who are living different lives. They bear the fruit of the Spirit But some get only snatches of victory. Once in a while they will have a day that seems to be a victorious day over temptation, but then they slide right back into tht same old rut of living, and hunger and long for the righteousness of daily growth.

There are other Christians who have never really learned the biblical truth of separation: separation from unclean thoughts and unclean habits.

There are some Christians who have learned little of a daily devotional life.

Surrender and Devotion

Some time ago a policeman asked me what the secret of victorious living was. I told him that there is no magic formula that can be pronounced. If any word could describe it, I would say *surrender*. The second word I would use would be *devotion*.

Nothing can take the place of a daily devotional life with Christ. The great missionary, Hudson Taylor, said, "Never mind how great the pressure is—only where the pressure lies. Never let it come between you and the Lord, then the *greater* the pressure, the more it *presses you* to His heart!" Our quiet time, our prayer time, the time we spend in the Word is absolutely essential for a happy Christian life. We cannot possible be happy, dynamic, and powerful Christians apart from a daily walk with Christ.

It is unfortunate that even in Christian circles our conversation is of comparatively small matters. We can quote the batting average of our favorite baseball star, but we are unable to quote a Bible verse other than John 3:16. We are full of talk about our homes, our cars, our television—but we are woefully ignorant of the things of God.

If a sick and dying man should stumble through our door, we would be incapable of guiding him through his problems to Christ the Savior.

Our spiritual intellects have become poverty-stricken; hence the trite verbal interchanges that pass between us. Our daily conversation when we meet each other, whether it be in the office or on the campus or in the shop, should be concerned with the things of God. We should be exchanging spiritual blessings and thoughts that we have received from our daily Bible reading.

It is not enough for us to have been confirmed, or to have made a decision for Christ at an altar, and to hope to walk in the glow of that experience successfully for the rest of our lives. Being human, we have to return and renew our commitment to God. We have to take inventory and get regular spiritual checkups.

Steps to Surrender

Christ is calling Christians today to cleansing, to dedication, to consecration, and to full surrender. It will make the difference between success and failure in our spiritual lives. It will make the difference between being helped and helping others. It will make a difference in our habits in our prayer life, in our Bible reading, in our giving, in our testimony, and in our church membership. This is the Christian's hour of decision!

But many ask, "How can I begin?" I would like to suggest that you take all of the sins that you are guilty of and make a list of them. Then confess them, and check them off, remembering that Jesus Christ forgives. The Bible says: "If we confess our sins, he is faithful and just to forgive us our sins, and to cleanse us from all unrighteousness" (1 John 1:9).

In addition, ask God to cleanse you from those sins you may not be aware of, and to make you more sensitive to the presence of hidden sins in your life—wrong motives, wrong attitudes, wrong habits, wrong relationships, wrong priorities. It may even be that you will have to make restitution if you have stolen anything, or you may have to seek out someone and ask his forgiveness for a wrong you have committed.

Then, after you have confessed every known sin in your life, yield every area of your life. Yield your girl friend, your boy friend, your family, your business, your career, your ambitions, your soul, the innermost thoughts and depths of your heart; yield them all to Christ. Hold nothing back. As the songwriter says: "Give them all to Jesus."

Take your eyes and your ears and your hands and your feet and your thoughts and your heart: give them completely and unreservedly to Christ. Then by faith believe that God has accepted your surrender.

Paul said: "I am crucified with Christ: nevertheless I live; yet not I, but Christ liveth in me" (Galatians 2:20).

We can reckon ourselves indeed dead unto sin. The Bible says we can be more than conquerors through Him who loved us.

The Secret of Surrender

It has been my privilege to know what it means to walk in the way of Christ. What a thrilling, joyous experience it is to wake up every morning and know His presence in the room! What a thrilling, joyous experience it is to know in the evening, when the sun is setting, the peace of God as you go to bed and to sleep the sleep of only those who know Christ! What a joy it is to walk in the eternal and permanent experience of Christ!

> *God is in every tomorrow,*
> *Therefore I live for today—Certain of finding at sunrise*
> *Guidance and strength for the way.*
> *Power for each moment of weakness,*
> *Hope for each moment of pain.*
> *Comfort for every sorrow,*
> *Sunshine and joy after rain!*

ANONYMOUS

And I know what it is to fall flat on my face. As Alexander Whyte, the great Scottish clergyman, said at the turn of the century, "Perseverance of the saints consists in ever new beginnings."

Do you hunger for such a walk? Do you long for such joy, peace, contentment, abandonment, and adventure in your own souls? Do you long to produce the fruit of the Spirit, which is "love, joy, peace, longsuffering, gentleness, goodness, faith, meekness, temperance" (Galatians 5:22, 23)? You can if you abide in Christ as the branch abides in the vine.

First, remember that the Christian life is lived by "Christ in you." However, if Christ does not have all of us, it is impossible to live a happy Christian experience. When He has all of us, then He fills us to overflowing and He produces in us the fruit of the Spirit. It is absolutely impossible for any person to manufacture, generate, or produce the Christian life apart from the power of the Holy Spirit. He stands at this moment ready to enter our hearts with a floodtide of blessing if we will surrender every area of our personalities and lives to Him. It is our birthright! We must claim it—believe it—accept it! It's ours *now*.

If this is your hunger and desire, then God will do exactly what He has promised to do: He will fill you. "Happy are they that hunger and thirst after righteousness: for they shall be filled." Every promise God has ever made He has kept. He will fill you now if you are hungry enough to surrender.

The Source of Righteousness

Second, God will fill you with His righteousness, because man has no holy longings, no holy cravings that cannot ultimately be satisfied.

We shall *not* be perfect in thought, word, and deed until we are glorified in the world to come, but the breath of that glory, and a godlikeness of character, is the Christian's proper heritage in this earthly walk. We are *Christians,* and the world should sense to its conviction that, wherever we walk in its midst, a heavenly virtue still goes out from whatever truly bears His Name.

People hunger for food, and God sends the sun and rain upon the golden fields of grain. The grain is made into flour and flour into bread, and our physical hunger is satisfied.

People hunger for love; and ideally they are born into a home where their parents love them. Later, perhaps, God ignites the fire of affection in another heart, and two hearts are made complete in the bonds of holy matrimony.

People hunger for knowledge, and God raises up institutions of learning. He calls out committed instructors and puts it into the hearts of the rich to endow these schools and students are satisfied in their thirst for knowledge.

People hunger for fellowship, and God allows engineers to build cities. There people can share their industry, their knowledge, and their skills.

Don't tell me that God can supply us with an abundance of everything material and yet will let us starve spiritually!

The Bible says: "Hearken diligently unto me, and eat ye

that which is good, and let your soul delight itself in fatness" (Isaiah 55:2).

Again the Bible says: "For the bread of God is he which cometh down from heaven, and giveth life unto the world" (John 6:33).

Satisfaction in Christ

Third, God will satisfy the hunger and thirst of those who desire His righteousness, because He loves the world with an undying affection. He moved heaven and earth to redeem us. Would it seem logical that a father would pay a huge ransom to redeem a son and then forsake him in his hour of hunger? The fact that the initial cost of our salvation was so great helps us know that God certainly does not desire that we shall want for anything. A parent who loves his child will not willingly see him starve.

The Bible says: "But my God shall supply all your need according to his riches in glory by Christ Jesus" (Philippians 4:19).

This promise, "Happy are they which do hunger and thirst after righteousness," is one which makes us responsible to God, and God responsible to us. Our small human part is to hunger and to thirst.

If we have no desire for righteousness, it means only that we have permitted sin and neglect to spoil our desire for fellowship with God. No matter how alluring, attractive, and pleasant the tidbits of the world may seem, they can never satisfy our deeper longings and heart cravings.

We can only know peace of heart and tranquillity of mind when we admit and confess our deeper hungers, when we yield completely to God and when we are willing to turn from the synthetic substitutes of the world and drink in the "water of life."

*Blessed are the merciful: for they shall
obtain mercy."*   Matthew 5:7

CHAPTER SIX

Happiness through Showing Mercy

THE BIBLE SAYS, "He that hath pity upon the poor lendeth
unto the Lord; and that which he hath given will he pay
again" (Proverbs 19:17). A group of businessmen had a hunt-
ing lodge. It was their custom to have devotions each evening.
One night they called on the godly mountain caretaker to
lead in prayer. "O Lord," he prayed, "have mercy on us, 'cause
mercy suits our case." In the Bible mercy refers to compassion, to pity for the undeserving and the guilty. Perhaps no
more beautiful illustration of it exists in the Bible (apart from
God's mercy to us in Christ) than that of Joseph and his undeserving brothers.

You recall how, through jealousy, the brothers sold Joseph
into slavery, convincing his father that he had been devoured
by wild beasts. In the following years Joseph through his faith-
fulness to God and his masters, rose in position in Egypt
until he was second in power to Pharaoh himself.

It was famine that drove the unsuspecting brothers down to Egypt to buy food. Read again the incredible story of Joseph recognizing his brothers, his compassionate dealing with them, how he got them to bring his old father and move with their families to Egypt where he could nourish them through the remaining years of famine. Where vengeance and just retribution were certainly justified, Joseph showed only mercy and lovingkindness.

In fact, he says to his apprehensive brothers (in Genesis 50), ". . . you thought evil against me; but God meant it unto good. . . . Now therefore fear ye not: I will nourish you, and your little ones. And he comforted them, and spake kindly unto them" (vv. 20–21).

What mercy!

So, too, in our lives, we might be prompted to be merciful to those who have wronged us, hurt us, or even done incredibly cruel things to us. If we were submissive and loyal to God we could see behind the unkindness and evil God's love working for our good and His glory.

We have a contrasting story in the rich young ruler who, when told by Jesus to go and sell all he had and give to the poor, then come and follow Him, went away sorrowful for he had great possessions (Matthew 19:22). Here an opportunity to show mercy was held back by greed.

The rich young ruler thought possessions would bring him happiness—but they didn't. And yet he was unwilling to turn to Christ, the only true source of lasting happiness. He could not show mercy to others because of his selfishness and greed—and so he "went away sorrowful," never experiencing true happiness and fulfillment. "Happy are the merciful."

Jesus knew that one of the real tests of our yieldedness to God is our willingness to share with others. If we have no mercy toward others, that is one proof that we have never experienced God's mercy.

Mercy Is Not Self-centered

To paraphrase this Beatitude we might say, "They which have obtained mercy from God are so happy that they are merciful to others." Our attitude toward our fellowmen is a more accurate gauge of our religion than all of our religious rantings.

Alexander Pope prayed:

> Teach me to feel another's woe
> To hide the fault I see;
> That mercy I to others show,
> That mercy show to me.

Emerson must have been reading the gauge of human mercy when he said: "What you are speaks so loud that I cannot hear what you say."

Jesus summed up the whole matter of genuine Christianity when He said: "If any man thirst, let him come unto me, and drink. He that believeth on me, as the Scripture hath said, out of his inmost soul flow rivers of living water" (John 7:37, 38).

Christianity is, first, a coming to Christ—an inflowing of the Living Water; second, it is a reaching toward others—an outflowing. It is to be shared in love, mercy, and compassion with others.

A body of water which has an inlet but no outlet becomes a stagnant pond. When we think of Christianity as *my* experience, *my* emotions, *my* ecstasy, *my* joy, *my* faith—with no desire to share mercifully with others—we can only boast of stagnation. Not living, vital, flowing Christianity!

The Scripture says: "Defend the poor and fatherless: do justice to the afflicted and needy" (Psalm 82:3). "Whoso stoppeth his ears at the cry of the poor, he also shall cry himself, but shall not be heard" (Proverbs 21:13).

Jesus said: "Give to him that asketh thee, and from him that would borrow of thee turn not thou away (Matthew 5:42). And: "Give, and it shall be given unto you; good measure, pressed down, and shaken together, and running over, shall men give into your bosom" (Luke 6:38).

In this Beatitude, which we could well term the "outflowing" Beatitude, Jesus is emphasizing the fact that we are to be unchoked channels through which His love and mercy flow out to other people.

If we have a religion which does not work effectively in everyday life, one which fails to condition our attitudes toward our fellow men and one which makes us spiritual introverts, we may be sure that we do not know the Christ who spoke these Beatitudes!

Satan does not care how much you theorize about Christianity or how much you profess to know Christ. What he opposes vigorously is the way you live Christ—the way you become an instrument of mercy, compassion, and love through which He manifests Himself to the world. If Satan can take the mercy out of Christianity, he has killed its effectiveness. If he can succeed in getting us to talk a good case of religion but to live a poor one, he has robbed us of our power.

If we embrace a spiritual, aesthetic gospel only and disregard our obligation to our fellow men, we annul it all. The gospel of the New Testament can come into full blossom only when the seed of the Spirit is buried in the rich soil of human mercy.

It is first an intaking, and then an outgiving. Jesus said in our outgiving we would find happiness.

Some time ago a lady wrote and said, "I am sixty-five years old. My children are all married, my husband is dead, and I am one of the loneliest people in all the world." It was suggested to her that she find a way of sharing her religious faith and her material goods with those around her. She wrote a few weeks later and said, "I am the happiest woman in town. I have found a new joy and happiness in sharing with others."

That's exactly what Jesus promised!

Mercy in Action

What are some of the areas in today's world toward which we can show mercy?

FIRST: We can show mercy by *caring for the needs of others*. We should look around at our neighbors and see if any are hurting or in need.

Who is my neighbor? He who is closest to me—my husband or wife, child, parent, brother, sister, the person next door, the couple down the street. It is easier to be concerned with the deprived person halfway around the world, and ignore the needs of those closest to me—perhaps only a word of encouragement or appreciation. At the same time, we cannot ignore the needs of our fellowmen on a worldwide scale.

When I go to bed tonight, I must remember that over half of the world's population is hungry, poor, and wretched. Most of these are illiterate people who are unable to read or write. Most use farming methods a thousand years old. Many are little better than slaves to the big landlords who own the land. Others live in countries with corrupt or oppressive governments. Their lives are burdened with injustice or prejudice, and they have little opportunity to get ahead. Their lives are marked by hopelessness and despair. They need food, education, clothes, homes, medical care, and—most of all—love. We have a responsibility to these downtrodden peoples of the world.

Did not Jesus feed the multitudes as well as preach the gospel to them? Did He not point out to us the folly of talking religion and failing to put it into action? Did He not say: "Woe unto you, scribes and Pharisees, hypocrites! for ye shut up the kingdom of heaven against men. . . . for ye devour widows' houses, and for a pretense make long prayer: therefore ye shall receive the greater damnation" (Matthew 23:13, 14)?

A young man from our community is a skilled helicopter pilot. He undoubtedly could make a very high salary working for a major corporation, but instead he has joined a small Christian mission which uses helicopters to reach remote areas of the world with the gospel and with relief supplies. Much of his work has been in some of the drought-stricken areas of Africa, where millions of people live on the brink of starvation every day. Recently he wrote, "I often feel at a loss of words to describe some of the conditions in places here. Some I don't want to describe—just forget." But then he added, "The rewards are high here in seeing our efforts really helping people." In the midst of terrible, heartbreaking conditions he has discovered the truth of Jesus' words: "Happy are the merciful."

How can we theorize about religion and debate doctrinal matters while the world is dying in misery without the necessities of life and, in many cases, without hope?

What a selfish and ingrown people we have become! Little wonder that there is so much boredom, frustration, and unhappiness. The words of Jesus, "Happy are the merciful," are certainly applicable to us.

The late Dr. Frank Laubach once wrote me, "In my opinion, the United States must make an all-out effort to help the destitute half of the world out of its misery, or we shall find that the world has gone Communist because of our neglect."

Most of us cannot go to these faraway lands, but we can give to missionary and charitable causes that will help build hospitals, educational institutions, and orphanages—and provide the necessities of life to many of these destitute millions.

But let's come closer home. If we only looked, we would find people near us who are in physical need. One Christmas

Eve a friend came to my house and said, "Would you like to go out with me distributing Christmas packages up in the mountains?" I was glad to go. And I was in for one of the greatest surprises of my life! I thought everybody in our community had all the necessities of life. But I was taken back into some little mountain valleys where people did not have enough to wear, enough to eat, and could not even afford soap to wash their bodies. Appalled and humbled, I asked God to forgive me for neglecting the people in my own community. I had not even bothered to look around me to see what people's needs were.

If we will ask God to show us, we will find people in our own communities who need physical help.

There are others in our community who need a friend. There are many lonely people who never know the hand-clasp of a friend. They never receive a letter. They sit isolated in their loneliness. Having an interested friend willing to write to them and to visit with them would change their entire lives. One of the happiest women in our church lives alone but makes a habit of visiting nursing homes. She reads to the patients, wheels them to the gift shop and cafeteria. When my mother had very few visit her from her church, this dear woman was faithful to her weekly. She is happy in a ministry in nursing homes.

There are others who are lonely and miserable because they perhaps do not have personalities that lend themselves to mixing with other people. I have a friend who went to a social gathering. A harelipped lad with pimples on his face sat over in the corner. No one paid any attention to him. He looked lonely, despondent, and miserable, and completely out of place. My friend went over and spent the evening with him. When he left, the lad was full of smiles. This friend had shown mercy.

There are a thousand little ways that we can be merciful in our daily lives. There may be a hospital nearby which we could visit. There are scores of people on hospital beds who long for someone to call on them, to bring them flowers and a cheery smile. We can show mercy by visiting the sick.

Prejudice—A Barrier to Mercy

SECOND: We can show mercy by *doing away with our prejudices.*

All over the world a new nationalism is rising. Color bars are being broken down while other social barriers are being raised. Prejudice stalks many countries.

I have been privileged across the years to visit many, many countries in every part of the world. However, I have never visited a country which did not have some problem with prejudice. At times it was prejudice against a racial or religious minority within its boundaries. At times it was prejudice against people from other nations. At times it was prejudice or resentment against those who were wealthier or those who were poorer than the average. But prejudice is a universal problem. Why? One reason is because prejudice has its roots in pride—and pride is at the heart of sin. Just as sin is universal, so prejudice is universal as long as our hearts are untouched by God's regenerating power.

The word *prejudice* means "prejudging" or "making an estimate of others without knowing the facts." Prejudice is a mark of weakness, not of strength; it is a tool of the bigot, but never a device of the true Christian. One of our great problems in this complex age continues to grow since modern man has forsaken the pathway of Christian mercy and understanding—and has chosen to walk the road of intolerance and intrigue. Someone has said, "Prejudice is being down on what you're not up on." Lack of awareness along with prejudice stifles mercy.

Edwin Markham referred to the prevailing gentility of yesteryear when he said:

> *He drew a circle that shut me out,*
> *Heretic, rebel, a thing to flout;*
> *But Love and I had the wit to win,*
> *We drew a circle that took him in.*

Prejudice is measured by computing the distance between our own biased opinions and the real truth. If we would all be perfectly honest before God, there would be no prejudice. But since most of us by nature are possessed of biased minds and perverted hearts, prejudice is widespread in the world.

The late Edward R. Murrow once said, "There is no such thing as an objective reporter. We are all slaves of our environment."

All of us have personal biases and prejudices. Despite our improved educational system, our prejudices have grown in the past few years—so we can conclude that education is not the cure for all prejudice.

Even the great Charles Lamb once said: "I am, in plainer words, a bundle of prejudices, made up of likings and dislikings."

Prejudice is a form of robbery, for it robs its victim of a fair trial in the court of reason. It is also a murderer, because it kills the opportunity of advancement for those who are its prey.

Jesus struck at the very core of it when He said: "And why beholdest thou the mote that is in thy brother's eye, but considerest not the beam that is in thine own eye" (Matthew 7:3). And then He laid down a specific rule against it when He said: "Judge not, that ye be not judged" (Matthew 7:1).

I seriously doubt if we would be prejudiced against anyone if we had all the facts in hand. We are quick to judge and prone to denounce that which we do not understand or know or experience.

Often prejudice would vanish if we had all the facts in hand. We also would be less quick to judge if we would put ourselves in the place of other people, understanding their background, sensing their problems, sympathizing with their weaknesses. Yes, education can do much to neutralize our prejudices—and yet we often find that when we apparently have conquered one type of prejudice, another type crops up in our hearts which is just as strong. I have known people who were able to overcome prejudices against people of another race—and yet their hearts were filled with scorn and prejudice against people of their own race who were of a different social class or a different political party.

The Antidote to Prejudice

But how can we get rid of this murderous prejudice? There is only one way we can get rid of prejudice: by the process of spiritual rebirth through faith in Christ. Only then do we discover God's love for all humanity, and only then will we begin to look at others through the eyes of God and see them as He sees them. Only then does God's love begin to take root in our hearts, pushing out the hate and indifference and selfishness that have resided there. In myself I do not have the capacity to love others as I should, but "The fruit of the Spirit is love" (Galatians 5:22). Yes, Christ can give us a love for others we would never have otherwise, "because the love of God is shed abroad in our hearts by the Holy Ghost which is given unto us" (Romans 5:5). This is an operation which only God can perform.

Listen to the words of Saul of Tarsus, once one of the world's most prejudiced men: "Love suffereth long, and is kind; love envieth not; love vaunteth not itself, is not puffed up. . . . Rejoiceth not in iniquity, but rejoiceth in the truth; Beareth all things, believeth all things, hopeth all things, endureth all things" (1 Corinthians 13:4–7).

What the logic of Greece could not do for Saul, the grace of God did. What the culture of Rome could not do, the grace of God accomplished. After his experiences on the Damascus road, Paul found his old prejudices melting away. *Mercy* became the key word of his preaching, the theme of his Epistles, and the pattern for his conduct. "I beseech you therefore . . . by the mercies of God, that ye present your bodies a living sacrifice" (Romans 12:1) was the theme of his pleadings. Having received mercy, he was an exponent of mercy. Having been delivered from his own prejudices, he was eager that all might find release from their destructive power.

How can we be so brazen as to be prejudiced against a person when God in His mercy has been so merciful toward us?

Go with the Gospel

THIRD: We can show mercy by *sharing the gospel of Christ* with others.

Man's spiritual poverty is even more wretched than his physical poverty. His failure to do what he ought to do and be what he ought to be proves that there is something inherently wrong with him.

The Bible puts it this way: "The heart is deceitful above all things, and desperately wicked" (Jeremiah 17:9). All immorality wantonness, greed, selfishness, prejudice, suffering, hatred, and bigotry stem from one source: the human heart. Nothing in the universe has fallen lower, and yet by the grace of God nothing can rise higher.

Physical poverty, of course, is more visible and apparent to us. We are touched by pictures of those who are starving or who live in rat-infested slums or on the street—and we should be. But spiritual poverty is much more difficult to see, because we only see it as we look at the world through the "spectacles" of God's Word. I have a friend who is extremely near-sighted. Even objects only a few feet away are a blur to him, and if he were to look across a valley, for example, he would be unable to tell you if it had houses or trees on the other side. But when he puts on his glasses it is a different store! Then his vision is almost as sharp as that of an airline pilot. In the same way, the spiritual poverty of the world is not clear or even evident to us until we begin to look at it in the light of God's Word, the Bible. But when we begin to understand God's Word, we realize that the world is lost and under the judgment of God apart from Christ.

Some people have said, "Oh, well, it does not really matter what people believe, just so they are sincere. Somehow all paths lead eventually to God, I guess. And if God is a loving God, then everyone will be saved eventually whether they are trusting Christ or have rejected Him." But the Bible says otherwise. "Neither is there salvation in any other: for there is none other name under heaven given among men, whereby we must be saved" (Acts 4: 12).

The fact that after two thousand years of Christianity more than half of the world's population still knows nothing about the saving, transforming grace of Christ should stir us to a renewed dedication to tell a dying world about the mercy of God.

Jesus said: "Go ye into all the world, and preach the gospel to every creature" (Mark 16:15).

Notice the little word *go*. A little word—but worldwide in its sweep! The apostles first had to *come*, and now Jesus commands them to *go*!

We have come in this generation and stopped short, but Christ says, "Go." A little word—but wrapped up in this little word is the whole sum and substance of Christ's gospel. "Go" is the first part of the word "gospel." It should be the watchword of every true follower of Christ. It should be emblazoned on the banners of the Church. "Go," says the Master. Nearly two thousand years have dragged their weary lengths down the road of time, and yet millions of people are sitting in spiritual darkness.

Is There Any Other Remedy?

There are two opposing concepts about man's true nature. Some assert that human nature is basically good and may rise to higher and higher levels of excellence apart from God. Humanity's basic problem, according to this view, is simply ignorance or unfavorable social or economic conditions. If people can be educated enough and if their social and economic situation is right, then selfishness and conflict will be eliminated. This makes a powerful appeal to our pride, for we do not want to think that we are unable to rise above ourselves. But human experience has repeatedly shown otherwise. Yes, education is important; God, after all, is the author of all truth, and in Christ "are hid all the treasures of wisdom and knowledge" (Colossians 2:3). But lust, greed, and selfishness remain firmly entrenched in our hearts, no matter how much education we have or how ideal our social conditions may be.

The other concept of human nature is that of the Bible. It holds that man was created in the image of God, and as such was originally perfect—exactly the way God intended him to be. But humanity turned its back on God, choosing to be independent of Him. And when they did, something radical and devastating happened to the human heart.

However, today there are statesmen who assume that better organized human government is the remedy for the world's dilemma. They assume that inasmuch as vice and crime flow from ignorance and poverty that virtue could issue from knowledge and competence. Yet history proves this theory inadequate. Constitutional and statutory law lacks the essential element to purify human nature. The power is not within the province of law, whether human or divine.

The Bible says: "By the deeds of the law there shall no flesh be justified in his sight" (Romans 3:20). Again: "What the law could not do, in that it was weak . . . God sending his own Son in the likeness of sinful flesh . . . condemned sin in the flesh" (Romans 8:3).

All of us agree that one form of government may be better than another, but all forms of government have been inadequate to suppress vice and give universal prevalence to virtue to change human nature. Rome was no more pure under the eloquent Cicero than under the cruel Nero.

History proves that it is impossible to solve the problem of human nature by civil law. That is not to say of course, that laws against evil are unnecessary or unimportant—quite the opposite. The Bible says in fact that God has given to civil government the authority to punish wrongdoing, and we are to support justice and the common good of society. "For rulers are not a terror to good works, but to the evil"

(Romans 13:3). Good government is also to work for the positive good of society.

But all too often we think that some particular form of government will solve all our problems. Some tyrants and dictators will do all they can to impose their type of government or their political philosophy on other nations, by force or subversion if necessary. Yes, some forms of government are certainly better than others—and one reason is that they have a better understanding of the limitations and possibilities of human nature. Government and civil laws are somewhat like the cages in a zoo—they can restrain evil and keep it from getting out of hand, but they cannot change the basic nature of the human heart.

As an American, I rejoice in our liberties and the legal safeguards we have against those who would seek to destroy society.

But our government is certainly going to fall like a rope of sand if unsupported by the moral fabric of God's Word. The moral structure in our country grew from Judeo-Christian roots. When those values are applied, they produce moral fruits. But if that structure disappears, the moral sentiment that shapes our nation's goals will disappear with it.

Then also, there is the person who claims that the remedy for vice is to be found in a universal system of education. His opinion is that man will be made pure and happy by intellectual culture and mental repose.

Suppose that education is the answer to all the problems that man faces. Develop the intellectual to the maximum; yet do you get virtue? Knowledge did not save Solomon from vice or Byron from immorality. Art and education may refine the taste: but they cannot purify the heart, forgive sin, and regenerate the individual. The Holocaust was carried out by educated people, some brilliantly so. It could well be called a demonstration of educated depravity.

A few years ago my wife and I visited the Nazi death camp of Auschwitz, located in southern Poland. Here some six million people—both Jews and non-Jews from throughout Europe—were brutally imprisoned and murdered. We saw the barbed wire, the instruments of torture, the airless punishment cells, the gas chambers and crematorium. Every square foot of that terrible place was a stark and vivid witness to man's inhumanity to man. We laid a memorial wreath and then knelt to pray at a wall in the midst of the camp where 20,000 people had been shot. When I got up and turned around to say a few remarks to those who had gathered with us, my eyes blurred with tears and I almost could not speak. How could such a terrible thing happen—planned and carried out by people who were often highly educated? The problem is the human heart. Jesus declared, "For out of the heart proceed evil thoughts, murders, adulteries, fornications, thefts, false witness, blasphemies" (Matthew 15:19).

It is not simply education in civilization that the world is wanting today, but civilization with enlightened conscience; not simply institutions and airlines and gigantic corporations, but all these entities free from graft and taint of every kind. Yet today an educated, civilized society is turning its face while thousands of unborn babies are being killed. God Himself, if not history, will judge this greater holocaust.

Where is mercy?

I would rather have a world filled with ignorant savages than with civilized sophisticates without morality. Better the wild, unexplored wilderness than the debauched palace of civilized shame. Better the cannibal of the South Seas than the civilized vultures of our cities.

The mathematician can solve problems on paper but can he solve his personal problems? The orthopedic surgeon can set broken bones but what can he do for a broken heart? The engineer can read the blueprints but where is his blueprint for daily living?

Reformed by Regeneration

Should we drive out civilization? you ask. No, we should pray God to *reform* it *by regeneration*. Starve out graft and put in honesty. Drive out prejudice and put in the Golden Rule. Drive out ruthlessness and put in mercy. This can be done only through an acceptance of Jesus Christ as personal Savior on the part of individuals who make up the society of the world.

We can put a public school and a university in the middle of every block of every city in America—but we will never keep America from rotting morally by mere intellectual education. Education cannot be properly called education which neglects the most important aspects of man's nature. Partial education throughout the world is far worse than none at all if we educate the mind but not the soul.

Turn a half-educated man loose upon the world, put him in the community with inexhaustible resources at his command but recognizing no power higher than his own—he is a monstrosity! He is but halfway educated and is far more dangerous than if he were not educated at all. He is a speeding locomotive without an engineer. He is a tossing ship without a compass, pilot, or destiny.

To think of civilizing people without converting them to Christ is about as wise as to think about transforming wolves into lambs merely by washing them and putting on them a fleece of wool.

"Happy are the merciful: for they shall obtain mercy."

The mercy the world needs is the grace, love, and peace of our Lord Jesus Christ. It is His transforming and regenerating power that the world needs more than anything else.

To be sure, we are to use the world's physical resources, but along with them we are to take the regenerating power of Christ. We are to take a cup of cold water in one hand and regeneration in the other and give them to a physically and spiritually starved world. We have thought that man's needs were entirely physical, but we are beginning to realize that they are also spiritual.

The Gifts of the Gospel

The gospel of Christ provides for our *physical being*. Materialism can see nothing in our bodies except laboratory analyses, but the Bible with stern rebuke exclaims: "What? know ye not that your body is the temple of the Holy Spirit?" (1 Corinthians 6:19).

The gospel provides for our *intellect*. It stimulates the intellect to the highest activity. It commands the complete education of all our intellectual powers. The Bible instructs: "Gird up the loins of your mind" (1 Peter 1:13). It opens before a regenerated person a whole universe of truth.

The gospel also provides for our *sensibilities.* "Let not your heart be troubled" (John 14:1). "Blessed are they that mourn: for they shall be comforted," says Jesus. This is what humanity needs. Humanity wants comfort in its sorrow, light in its darkness, peace in its turmoil, rest in its weariness, and healing in its sickness and diseases: the gospel gives all of this to us.

The gospel provides for our *will.* It provides that we may yoke our will to the omnipotent will of God and thereby strengthen our own will.

The gospel also provides for man's *moral nature.* Its code of morals is acknowledged by any man to be above reproach.

The gospel also provides the only satisfaction in the universe for our *spiritual nature.* The gospel recognizes the tremendous fact of sin and proposes an adequate remedy.

It does not evade the age-old question, "What must I do to be saved?" by saying there is no need of salvation. It does not lift us out of the pit by telling us that we are not bad. It does not remove the sting of our conscience by taking away conscience itself. It does not haunt us.

The gospel shows people their wounds and bestows on them love. It shows them their bondage and supplies the hammer to knock away their chains. It shows them their nakedness and provides them the garments of purity. It shows them their poverty and pours into their lives the wealth of heaven. It shows them their sins and points them to the Savior.

This is the message we are to take to a lost, confused, and bewildered world! This is showing mercy!

There are those near us in our communities who need the regenerating power of Christ. We can call them by name. I suggest that each of us make a list and begin by spending time in prayer for these needy people. We should ask God to show us how to witness to them and how to win them. Their lives can be transformed by the message we give them. We are to share this gospel we have received. If Christ has done anything for us, then we must share it. In so doing, we are showing mercy!

William Shakespeare wrote:

> The quality of mercy is not strained;
> It droppeth as the gentle rain from heaven
> Upon the place beneath: it is twice blest
> It blesseth him that gives and him that takes:
> 'Tis mightiest in the mightiest; it becomes
> The throned monarch better than his crown.

No, the path to happiness is not found in selfish living and indifference to others. Instead, when we have experienced the mercy of God then we will show mercy to others. Then we will indeed be "twice blest" because we will both make others happy and experience true happiness ourselves. "Happy are the merciful: for they shall obtain mercy."

Blessed are the pure in heart: for they shall see God.   Matthew 5:8

CHAPTER SEVEN

Happiness in Purity

IN THE BIBLE the heart is considered to be something far more complex than a bodily organ. It is called the seat of the emotions. Fear, love, courage, anger, joy, sorrow, and hatred are ascribed to the heart. It has come to stand for the center of the moral, spiritual, and intellectual life of a person. The "heart" is said to be the seat of a person's conscience and life.

Jesus said, "Happy are the pure in heart." Now, we should be able to take that for just what it means. If the heart is the seat of affection, then our love toward God must be pure. If the heart is the center of our motives, then our motives must be pure. If the heart is the residence of our wills, then our wills must be yielded to Christ. We are to be pure in love, pure in motive, and pure in desire.

It might be well to pause at this point to observe just what is meant by being "pure in heart."

The True Meaning of Purity

The word which is translated "pure" here was used in several ways in the original Greek language. For one thing, it was often used to mean something that was unadulterated or unmixed with anything foreign, such as pure gold which has not been mixed with any other metal, or milk which has not been watered down. Or again, it often simply meant "clean," like a dish which had been thoroughly washed or clothes that had been scrubbed.

Now apply those meanings to "pure in heart." If we are truly pure in our hearts, we will have a singleminded devotion to the will of God. Our motives will be unmixed, our thoughts will not be adulterated with those things which are not right. And our hearts will be clean, because we will not tolerate known sin in our hearts and allow it to pollute us. We will take seriously the Bible's promise, "If we say that we have no sin, we deceive ourselves, and the truth is not in us. If we confess our sins, he is faithful and just to forgive us our sins, and to cleanse us from all unrighteousness" (1 John 1:8–9).

There is, however, another dimension to this word "pure." It also sometimes meant something which was purged of wrong so it could be used for right. William Barclay points out that it could be used of an army which had been purged or cleared of soldiers who were cowardly or weak and unable to fight. It would then be a "pure" army, filled with dedicated and trained soldiers ready for battle. This would be like a person's body which is purified of sickness so it is strong and able to work. In the same way, when we are "pure in heart" we are ready to do those good things which God has for us to do.

In other words, purity of heart has both a negative and a positive side. On one hand, our hearts are to be emptied of sin and its dominion over us. On the other hand, we are to be pure in our actions and filled with all that is pure. The Bible illustrates these negative and positive sides to purity: "*Put to death* therefore what is earthly in you: fornication, impurity, passion, evil desire, and covetousness. . . . *put them all away:* anger, wrath, malice, slander, and foul talk. . . . *Put on then,* as God's chosen ones, holy and beloved, compassion, kindness, lowliness, meekness, and patience. . . . And above all these *put on* love" (Colossians 3:5,8,12,14, RSV, emphasis added).

Misconceptions about Purity of Heart

Did Jesus mean that we were to attain a sinless perfection, a spiritual state in which it would be impossible for us to fail again? No.

To be pure in heart does not mean that I must live in a straitjacket, looking pious and retreating periodically into monastic seclusion. Jesus denounced the Pharisees because they had a false conception of heart purity. He said: "Woe unto you, scribes and Pharisees, hypocrites! for ye are like unto whited sepulchres, which indeed appear beautiful outward, but are within full of dead men's bones, and of all uncleanness" (Matthew 23:27).

Jesus' debate with the Pharisees was right at this point.

They avowed that the favor of God was gained by making clean the outside of the cup, by observing certain religious rites, and by keeping the letter of the law. In other words, they worked from the "outside in" rather than from the "inside out."

But this was not God's plan. This did not produce purity of heart. This did not bring about happiness of soul.

Their superficial religion was powerless to cleanse their hearts from their moral filth and corruption; hence the Pharisees were not happy men. They were full of resentments bitternesses, prejudices, and hatreds. Why? Simply because they had lost sight of God's conception of the pure in heart. They thought that as long as they kept the letter of the law that this was enough.

But Jesus taught that God looks deeper than the outside actions of an individual. He searches and ponders the heart. God judges not so much the outside as He does the inside. He looks to the motives, thoughts, and intents of our heart.

We called one of our daughters "Bunny." She was a sweet, loving, cooperative child. At that time, many years ago, she was at the age where she was obsessed with the desire to help Daddy. Whatever I did, she would say, "Daddy, let me help you." Now Bunny meant well, but between you and me, she was seldom of any valuable assistance in a constructive way. If she helped me weed the flowers, she pulled up the flowers instead of the weeds. If she helped me unload the groceries, she invariably dropped something of value and broke it. If she helped me clean my study, she made a mess of things in general. But Bunny's motive was good—she

134

really wanted to help. So I tried to encourage this good, though undeveloped trait, realizing Bunny's motives. Incidentally, she has grown up to be an extraordinarily helpful, caring person.

This is exactly what God does. He does not judge the superficial goodness or the superficial badness of what we do. He goes deeper into the soul and probes as a surgeon! When God is through probing our hearts, He says: "The heart is deceitful above all things, and desperately wicked: who can know it?" (Jeremiah 17:9).

Evil in the Heart

When Jesus had finished probing the hearts of the people with whom He came in contact, He said: "Out of the heart of men proceed evil thoughts, adulteries, fornications, murders, thefts, covetousness, wickedness, deceit, lasciviousness, an evil eye, blasphemy, pride, foolishness" (Mark 7:21, 22). Jesus taught that the human heart was far from God: darkened, unbelieving, blind, proud, rebellious, idolatrous, and stony. He taught that the human heart in its natural state is capable of any wickedness and any crime.

A teenage boy was arrested in New York for having committed one of the most vicious murders of our time. His mother exclaimed, "But he is a good boy!" She had not stopped to realize that an unregenerate human heart is potentially capable of any crime. A certain poet has written:

> Quicken my conscience till it feels
> The loathsomeness of sin.

That is the reason why many of the peace treaties which have been signed in human history have not been kept and war has ensued. These treaties have been signed in good faith, but they were signed on the basis of trusting the motives of the other party. They have been broken time after time and millions have died on the battlefields of the world because the human heart is deceitful and desperately wicked.

Our hearts are impure! As a result, we are filled with inner tension, pride, frustration, confusion, and a thousand and one other spiritual, mental, and physical ills. The very root of our lives is bad. The theologian, William G. T. Shedd, said, "Human character is worthless, in proportion as abhorrence of sin is lacking in it."

Jesus says we will never be completely and supremely happy until our hearts are pure. Samuel Rutherford urged us to "Labor for a strong and lively sense of sin . . . the more sense of sin, the less sin."

The Cure for a Sick Heart

But if we have bad hearts, what can we do about them? "Should we try to reform or improve our hearts in some way?" someone asks.

Man—ever intent to live independently of God and His transforming grace—claims that environment, education, and right mental attitudes can change the heart and make it pure. "Put people in a wholesome atmosphere and they will be good," the humanist argument goes.

Although this may sound perfectly logical—like a good

many man-made theories—it simply will not hold water. Put an African baboon in a Boston drawing room, and how long will it take for him to act like a human being? "But that is twisting the argument," our humanist friends will object.

I think not! For we are dealing with the problem of nature as opposed to environment. The nature of an animal is affected by environment but can never be radically and essentially changed by it. An animal trainer may subdue that wild nature to a degree, but the baboon will always have the nature of a baboon, regardless of training and environment. Furthermore, the first crime, Cain's murder of Abel, was committed in a perfect environment!

There are others who say that our mental attitude toward life needs to be changed: "If we *think* right, we *are* right." To them the problem of evil is a psychological one. "Think positively," they say. "As a man thinketh in his heart, so is he."

This is all very good, and I have a great deal of sympathy for those who are trying through psychological means to help bring about better mental attitudes. But this also gives encouragement to the people who say, "Goody, goody. We can help ourselves, just as we had always thought." The "do-it-yourself" rage is spreading everywhere, and people are being told that to be happy all they have to do is to think "happiness thoughts." Such thoughts might cheer us, but they will never change us.

However, God says that our need is deeper-seated than the mind. He did not say, "Blessed are they who think happiness thoughts." He said: "Blessed are the pure in heart: for they shall see God."

This heart purity is not produced by mental suggestion, by environment or by education. It is a miracle wrought by God Himself. God says: "A new heart also will I give you, and a new spirit will I put within you: and I will take away the stony heart out of your flesh" (Ezekiel 36:26).

Purity of heart is a result of a rebirth, a miracle, a new creation. As the Bible says: "Which were born, not of blood, nor of the will of the flesh, nor of the will of man, but of God" (John 1:13).

We need cleansed, forgiven, justified, new hearts! Such can be received only as an act of God on the ground of the death of Christ on the cross.

A Sunday school teacher once told a class of boys and girls that nothing was impossible with God. One little boy objected, saying that he knew one thing God could not do.

"And what could that be?" asked the astonished teacher.

"To see my sins through the blood of Jesus Christ," the youngster wisely answered.

When we have properly confessed and renounced our sins and by faith received Christ into our hearts, then we receive a new heart from God. Only then can we be called "pure in heart." Only then can we know the secret of happiness!

Again, I should like to emphasize that this is not an emotional experience, though emotion may be a factor. I may not "feel" that I have a new heart but I can accept the fact by faith. Faith goes beyond logic, rationalization, and understanding. You may not be able to accept intellectually all that has been said on these pages, but I challenge you to believe and accept by faith that which you cannot understand. There would be no need for faith if we could understand all about God.

Jesus insisted that we must become as little children before we could enter the kingdom of heaven. Each of us must become as a little child and by faith grasp that which we cannot altogether understand. But on the other hand, realize that God can be trusted. Faith is not a blind leap in the dark! It is instead based squarely on what God has done for us in Jesus Christ. Our faith has a firm foundation, because it is not based on speculation or wishful thinking, but upon God and His Word. God can be trusted to keep His promises to us.

Certainly purity of heart is a prerequisite to entering the kingdom of heaven. There is no chance of a person's ever going to heaven until that one has received purity of heart. This purity of heart comes as an act of God after one has renounced sin and received Christ!

Have you received a new heart? If you have, then you stand on the threshold of discovering the secret of happiness!

It is impossible to live pure lives until we have pure hearts. Many people today are trying to put the cart before the horse. They are teaching purity of motives, desires, and actions to old, deceitful hearts! No wonder we have ended up such moral failures in spite of our vaunted knowledge and psychological approaches. Pure motives, desires, and actions stem from pure hearts.

The Nature of the Pure Heart

If we have received a cleansed and pure heart from God we are expected to live a pure life. Theologically (as we have already seen in the chapter on "Happy though Hungry"), this is called "sanctification."

Pure hearts will be Christlike. It is God's desire that we be conformed to the image of His Son. If Christ lives within us and our bodies become the abode of the Holy Spirit, is it any wonder that we should be like Him? And just what do we mean by Christlike?

The Bible says: "Let this mind be in you, which was also in Christ Jesus" (Philippians 2:5). Jesus had a humble heart. If He abides in us, pride will never dominate our lives. Jesus had a loving heart. If He dwells within us, hatred and bitterness will never rule us. Jesus had a forgiving and understanding heart. If He lives within us, mercy will temper our relationships with our fellow men. Jesus had an unselfish heart. If He lives in us, selfishness will not predominate but service to God and others will come before our selfish interests. But even more, Jesus' one desire was to do His Father's will. This is the essence of Christlikeness—eager obedience to the Father's will.

You say, "That's a big order!" I admit that. It would be impossible if we had to measure up to Him in our own strength and with our own natural hearts.

Paul recognized that he could never attain this heart purity by his own striving. He said: "I can do all things *through* Christ which strengtheneth me" (Philippians 4: 13).

God hasn't left us alone, out on a limb! Jesus said to His disciples: "Lo, I am with you alway, even unto the end of the world" (Matthew 28:20). They did what they did because He was with them. They were nothing but a group of rough, unlettered men; but with Christ in their hearts they "turned the world upside down" (Acts 17:6).

Christ provided the possibility of purity by His death on the cross. We have seen that the righteousness and the purity of God are imputed to men who confess their sins and receive Christ into their hearts.

Webster defines purity: "Freedom from foreign admixture or deleterious matter. Cleanness; freedom from foulness or dirt. Freedom from guilt or the defilement of sin: innocence; chastity. Freedom from any sinister or improper motives or views."

Though all of these ideas are embraced in the term *purity*, they do not set up an absolute standard by which to judge what is foreign and what is not, what is sin and what is not. It is best to regard purity in the all-embracing connotation: complete conformity to the holiness of God.

The Scriptures continually ask us to strive after *physical, mental,* and *moral* purity. God says: "Be ye holy; for I am holy" (1 Peter 1:16). Further, the Scripture says that without holiness, "no man shall see the Lord" (Hebrews 12:14). Again the Scripture says: "Who shall ascend into the hill of the Lord? or who shall stand in his holy place? He that hath clean hands, and a pure heart; who hath not lifted up his soul unto vanity, nor sworn deceitfully" (Psalm 24:3, 4).

We are actually commanded in Scripture: "Keep thyself pure" (1 Timothy 5:22).

Physical Cleanliness

God wants us *to be pure in body.* This includes *physical* cleanliness.

Caverno says, "When one realizes that by uncleanness of person or property he may endanger the health or life of family or even of society about him—as in keeping conditions that develop typhoid fever—he begins to realize that there is a close tie between cleanliness and morals."

The ancient Jews strove for physical cleanliness on religious grounds; and although many of the Old Testament laws of purification have been abolished as detailed prescriptions for today, others are incorporated into our own way of life. The principle of physical cleanliness is still in force. In the Middle Ages, however, many Christians felt that not bathing was a sign of humility and the dirtier they became, the more holy they were!

Even in the poorest of circumstances a person can afford some soap and water. There is absolutely no excuse for a Christian's being unclean, unkempt, or slovenly. If you have a pure heart, you will also want to have a pure body.

Physical cleanliness means more than just keeping our bodies washed, however. For example, God has given us our bodies and we are to take care of them in every reasonable way we can. The apostle Paul commanded Christians to be pure in body and to take care of their bodies. "What? know ye not that your body is the temple of the Holy Ghost which is in you, which ye have of God, and ye are not your own? For ye are bought with a price: therefore glorify God in your body, and in your spirit, which are God's" (1 Corinthians 6:19–20).

We need to get proper exercise, and we need to eat properly. We need to realize also that there is a close relationship between our physical health and our spiritual, mental and emotional outlook. Science is discovering more and more the truth of what the Bible said centuries ago: "A merry heart maketh a cheerful countenance: but by sorrow of the heart the spirit is broken" (Proverbs 15:13). The Bible also states, "A merry heart doeth good like a medicine: but a broken spirit drieth the bones" (Proverbs 17:22). When David sinned against God he was burdened inside with his guilt, but it also affected him physically. Later he wrote, "When I kept silence, my bones waxed old through my roaring all the day long" (Psalm 32:3).

Moral Cleanliness

Being pure in body also includes *chastity*. Thus Paul says: "This is the will of God, even your sanctification, that ye should abstain from fornication . . ." (1 Thessalonians 4:3).

How often the Scriptures warn against the sins of adultery and fornication. It is significant that in many references Paul mentions "uncleanness" immediately after "fornication."

Our newspapers are filled with stories of immorality in various parts of the nation. In fact, immorality is glorified today. Some of the most popular TV programs are about the decadent rich!

Let me warn you: the Scripture teaches that God hates immorality!

For several centuries our civilization has often been caught in the crosscurrents of a number of different secular philosophies. Often these have gained popular acceptance for a time, and have had a great impact on our institutions, ideas, and values. Some, for example, have taught that there are no firm or absolute moral values by which we are to guide our lives. Instead, morals are relative; we are to do whatever we think is right for us, without worrying about God and His moral law. Such views, however, only lead to moral chaos—and chaos within our society as well. One lawyer told me recently that the vast majority of his clients are not concerned about the fact they have done wrong—all they are interested in is not getting caught!

Many have been convinced that the Bible is not God's revelation, that salvation is to come through man and not through Christ, and that morality is relative and not absolute. We may as well say the rules of the road are relative and not absolute. How would you like to land at an airport where the laws of aviation were relative?

The practical results of this intellectual acceptance of humanism and behaviorism have been a degeneration of morals and the abandonment of religious ideals. The wave of behavioristic psychology that swept our college campuses and permeated the high school classrooms is now ingrained in the way our youth are living. The ideal of purity is scorned, immorality is laughed at in school—"God is old-fashioned!" What else can we expect but that thousands of our young people are growing up to be immoral? The Bible warns time after time that no immoral nation can survive and no immoral individual shall enter the kingdom of God.

One of the Ten Commandments says: "Thou shalt not commit adultery" (Exodus 20:14). I am keenly aware that this delicate subject is no longer considered taboo by clergymen. The newspapers mention it, pornographic writers make it the theme of their writings, it is the theme of everyday gossip, children talk about it, and almost every magazine has discussions and pictures about it. And beyond all that, the Bible mentions it over and over again as one of the worst sins! So why in the name of all that is just, proper, and holy should not preachers sound the warning against it?

The Bible says time after time: "Thou shalt not commit adultery." What does this word *adultery* mean? It is derived from the same Latin root from which we get our word *adulterate* which means "corrupt; to make impure or to weaken."

Sin is not merely the use of that which is corrupt, but more often the misuse of that which is pure and good. So adultery can apply to many things. This sin was so terrible that under Jewish law it was punishable by death. Under the Roman law it was punishable by death. Under the Greek law it was punishable by death. And under God's law, the Bible says, it is punishable by spiritual death.

The Bible says: "She that liveth in pleasure is dead while she liveth" (1 Timothy 5:6) and "The wages of sin is death" (Romans 6:23). The Bible says we are to keep our bodies pure, we are to abstain from fleshly lust. This sin is a sin not only against the body but against God.

Pure in Our Minds

God also wants us *to be pure in mind*. William Barclay said: "Pure thoughts mean those thoughts which can be examined by the Holy Spirit." Paul said: "Whatsoever things are pure . . . think on these things" (Philippians 4:8).

Returning to the question of chastity, we note that Jesus said: "Ye have heard that it was said . . . Thou shalt not commit adultery: But I say unto you, That whosoever looketh on a woman to lust after her hath committed adultery with her already in his heart" (Matthew 5:27, 28).

You can commit immorality by *evil imaginations*. In Genesis 6:5 we read: "And God saw that the wickedness of man was great in the earth, and that every imagination of the thoughts of his heart was only evil continually." God is concerned with our imaginations, for they in a large measure determine what kind of persons we are to be.

Solomon said: "As [a man] thinketh in his heart, so is he" (Proverbs 23:7). If our thoughts are evil, then our acts will be evil. If our thoughts are godly, then our lives will be godly.

Robert Browning said: "Thought is the soul of the act." Ralph Waldo Emerson said: "Thought is the seat of action, the ancestor of every action is thought."

If God destroyed the world during Noah's time for its continual evil imaginations, is it not reasonable to believe that all of the sin, lust, and licentiousness rampant today grieves His heart just as it did in that day?

Many people dream of sin, imagine sin, and if granted the opportunity would indulge in sin. All they lack is the occasion to sin. So in the sight of God they are sinners as great as though they had actually committed immorality. All transgression begins with sinful thinking. We who have come to Christ for a pure heart, must guard against the pictures of lewdness and sensuality which Satan flashes upon the screens of our imaginations. We must select with care the books we read. I must choose discerningly the kind of entertainment I attend, the kind of associates with whom I mingle, and the kind of environment in which I place myself. I should no more allow sinful imaginations to accumulate in my mind and soul than I would let garbage collect in my living room.

Benjamin Franklin said: "It is easier to suppress the first desire than to satisfy all that follow it." St. Augustine said: "Purity of soul cannot be lost without consent." Ask God to cleanse your mind and keep it purified. This can be done through reading the Bible, daily prayer, and association with the right kind of people.

As we have seen, Jesus indicated that one can engage in immorality by a *look*. The Bible places the "lust of the eye" right along with other major sins. Listen: "For all that is in the world, the lust of the flesh, and the lust of the eyes, and the pride of life, is not of the Father, but is of the world" (1 John 2:16).

Peter spoke of having "eyes full of adultery" (2 Peter 2:14). No wonder Job said: "I made a covenant with my eyes; why then should I think upon a maid?" (Job 31:1).

Our eyes see only what our soul allows them to see. If one's heart is out of harmony with God and he has never been born again, the odds are that he will have a perverted, distorted view of life. Like Paul, the scales of lust and animal passion can fall from our eyes when we catch a vision of Christ. At this moment I can make a covenant with my eyes.

I can take my eyes and nail them to the cross until I can say, "They have been crucified with Christ, never again to lust."

Immorality can be engaged in by the *tongue*. The Scripture warns about evil communications that corrupt good manners. The psalmist said: "Set a watch, O Lord, before my mouth" (Psalm 141:3). Off-color jokes and dirty stories have no place in the Christian life. Thousands of people are engaging in immorality by the way they talk. Keep your talk pure. Ask God to purify your tongue.

I can engage in immorality by the way I *dress*. If women purposely dress to entice a man to sin, then they are guilty whether the act is committed or not. A girl said one day, "I came forward in your meeting and accepted Christ. A few nights later I was going to a party. I put on my dress. I looked in the mirror, and it seemed as though Jesus were looking at me. I went to my wardrobe and changed my dress. And now I dress as though Jesus were my escort each evening." Dress to please Christ—in all modesty and good taste.

I can engage in immorality while *reading* unclean books and looking at unclean pictures. Our newsstands today are so indecent that a Christian cannot look upon them without blushing, and yet thousands of people are buying unclean books and the wrong type of magazines. The same is true of our movie and TV screens. By feeding our lusts, we are sinning against God.

Many of you who are reading these pages have committed this terrible sin of breaking the Seventh Commandment.

You have been unfaithful to your wife or husband, or you young people have yielded to this temptation of illicit sex. You have become impure in regard to chastity. The prophet Malachi wrote:

> Yet ye say, Wherefore? Because the LORD hath been witness between thee and the wife of thy youth, against whom thou hast dealt treacherously: yet *is* she thy companion, and the wife of the covenant. And did not he make one? Yet had he the residue of the spirit. And wherefore one? That he might seek a godly seed. Therefore take heed to your spirit, and let none deal treacherously against the wife of his youth. For the LORD, the God of Israel, saith that he hateth putting away: for *one* covereth violence with his garment, saith the LORD of hosts: therefore take heed to your spirit, that ye deal not treacherously (2:14–16).

Although the Bible teaches that this sin leads to hell, there is good news! The woman at the well had broken this commandment, but Christ forgave her and met the need of her life. Mary Magdalene had broken this commandment, but Christ wonderfully met the need of her life and cleansed her from sin. The sinful woman who had been taken in adultery was brought to Jesus by the Pharisees, but He said: "Neither do I condemn thee: go, and sin no more" (John 8:11). He did not condone her, but neither did He condemn her, because she had trusted in Him. He sent her away redeemed and forgiven, but commanded her to sin no more. Christ will do the same for you if you will let Him.

Pure in Our Actions

Not only does God want us to be pure in body and pure in mind, but He wants us *to be pure in conduct*.

Paul says: "Let no corrupt communication proceed out of your mouth, but that which is good to the use of edifying, that it may minister grace unto the hearers" (Ephesians 4:29).

Jesus said to the Pharisees: "O generation of vipers, how can ye, being evil, speak good things? for out of the abundance of the heart the mouth speaketh. A good man out of the good treasure of the heart bringeth forth good things: and an evil man out of the evil treasure bringeth forth evil things. But I say unto you, That every idle word that men shall speak, they shall give account thereof in the day of judgment. For by thy words thou shalt be justified, and by thy words thou shalt be condemned" (Matthew 12:34–37).

Cursing, telling smutty stories, smearing the good name of another and referring irreverently to God and the Scriptures may be considered as coming under the expression *corrupt speech*. Our speech is to be clean, pure, and wholesome.

Under this rule of good conduct also come our associations. Paul says that evil companionships corrupt good morals (1 Corinthians 15:33). The Bible warns against being unequally yoked with unbelievers. This condemns all business, social, fraternal, and religious associations in which unchristian principles and practices govern. Concerning the latter, John says: "If there come any unto you, and bring not this doctrine, receive him not into your house, neither bid him God speed: For he that biddeth him God speed is partaker of his evil deeds" (2 John 10, 11).

Christians who are involved in associations that are evil and corrupt are asked to "come out from among them, and be ye separate . . . and touch not the unclean thing" (2 Corinthians 6:17). God promises that if we do this, He will receive us into His most intimate fellowship.

The Bible teaches that purity of conduct includes truthfulness. God's Word teaches that we should be truthful in our representations of ourselves. With what scorn Christ denounced the hypocrisy of the scribes and Pharisees! In the Sermon on the Mount, He rebuked all hypocritical giving, praying, and fasting.

We should also be truthful in speaking of our past achievements in our particular vocation. God does not ask us to understate the facts—that might even be untruthfulness—but neither does He want us to overrate our achievements or our gifts, either in thought or in speech. In the Septuagint (Greek) version of the Old Testament Proverbs 24:28 says, "Overstate not with thy lips."

Purity in the Marketplace

We are also to be truthful in our business affairs. All misrepresentations of the quality of our merchandise, all false weights and measures, all padding of expense accounts, all forging of checks and other legal papers, and all unjust alterations of accounts are sins of untruthfulness and indicate lack of purity. The farmer who puts his spoiled wheat between two layers of good wheat when he takes it to the market and the fruit grower who puts his best fruit on top in his measure are dishonest. The tourist who misrepresents an article that is subject to duty on entering the country and the taxpayer who does not supply all the desired information are dishonest.

Being pure in conduct also includes *honesty* and *integrity* in dealing with our fellow men. Employers in business are to give proper wages for work done, while employees are to put in a full hour's honest labor for the wages they receive. A Christian should be known in his or her neighborhood or place of business as an honest person—one who can be trusted.

Purity and Happiness Are Possible

Jesus said: "Blessed are the pure in heart."

Do you want to be happy? All right, apply this Beatitude to your heart. Take it to yourself. The pure in heart are the only ones who can know what it means to be supremely happy. Their hearts are pure toward God and, as a result, are pure toward their fellow men.

They are happy because in possessing Him who is All and in All, they envy no one's worldly goods. They are happy because they envy not another person's praise or another person's place in the sun. Because they are the enemy of no one, they regard no one as their enemy. The result is peace with God and the world. Because their sins have been freely forgiven, they freely forgive those who have wronged them. They are thus purged of contemptuous malice.

But the greatest happiness that comes to the pure in heart

is not only a proper relationship with others but a sublime relationship with God. "For they shall see God." The gates of Eden swing open once more. God and man walk together once again.

Dying to Dirt

From the old magazine *Hi Call* comes this story:

Visiting in a mining town, a young minister was being escorted through one of the coal mines. In one of the dark, dirty passageways, he spied a beautiful white flower growing out of the black earth of the mine. "How can there be a flower of such purity and beauty in this dirty mine?" the minister asked the miner. "Throw some of the coal dust on it and see," was the reply. The minister did so and was surprised that as fast as the dirt touched those snowy petals, it slid right off to the ground, leaving the flower just as lovely as before. It was so smooth that the dirt could not cling to the flower.

Our hearts can be the same way. We cannot help it that we have to live in a world filled with sin, any more than the flower could change the place where it was growing. But God can keep us so pure and clean that though we touch sin on every side, it will not cling to us. We can stand in the midst of it just as white and beautiful as that flower.

The secret of purity is God! The secret of seeing and knowing God is a pure heart . . . a pure heart comes from God! Get a pure heart, and you can be supremely happy— no matter what the circumstances!

*Blessed are the peacemakers: for they shall be
called the children of God.*   Matthew 5:9

CHAPTER EIGHT

Happiness through Peacemaking

THE PROBLEM of human strife is as old as man. It had its
beginning on the outskirts of Eden when Cain, driven by
envy, murdered his more devout brother, Abel. Men fought
then as now: primarily because strife was inherent in their
natures.

Jesus spoke prophetically of our times when He said:
"And ye shall hear of wars and rumors of wars . . . nation
shall rise against nation, and kingdom against kingdom . . ."
(Matthew 24:6, 7).

Someone has pointed out that over the past 4,000 years
there has been less than 300 years of peace. Yet one won-
ders, was that universal peace? It is more likely that down
through history there has always been a war, or wars, in various parts of the world. Even the most optimistic person is
forced to admit that there is something seriously wrong with
a world that has such a passion for destruction.

If a man were sent from Mars to report earth's major
business, he would in all fairness have to say that war was

the earth's chief industry. He would report that the nations of the world were vying with each other in a race to see which could make deadlier weapons and amass bigger nuclear arsenals. He would say that earth's people are too quarrelsome to get along with each other and too selfish to live peacefully together.

Dr. Robert Oppenheimer, who supervised the creation of the first atomic bomb, was asked to appear before a congressional committee. They asked him if there was any defense against this awesome new weapon of war. "Certainly," the great physicist replied.

"And that is—" someone asked.

The audience awaited the answer in subdued silence. "Peace," the eminent scientist replied softly.

The Search for Peace

But why is it that after these thousands of years of life on this planet we are no nearer peace than were the warring tribes of ancient history?

The world is desperately searching for peace. There are millions of people who would gladly give their right arms to find it. They would like to have peace—deep, inward, satisfying peace.

They also yearn for peace in our world—freedom from conflict and war, freedom from the hatred and strife which divide families and communities, and freedom from fear of the future, wondering when a computer will malfunction or a maniacal dictator will place his finger on the nuclear or biochemical button and wipe out civilization as we know it.

The world thinks peace would come if everyone made a lot of money, but people haven't found peace in possessions. They have thought the world would have peace if all arms were destroyed. Yet Cain killed Abel without a handgun. It is man's heart that is the problem.

Some thought peace could be found in a bottle, but they didn't find it there. It was an artificial peace, frequently leading to death. They thought one would find it in getting and accumulating a lot of knowledge, so they got all the degrees they could get, but still didn't find it. Some have searched the religions of the world, even exotic and mindwarping cults, but haven't found peace even there.

There are a thousand ways we've turned, trying to find peace, but we haven't found it. We've escaped from reality for a few moments, for a few hours, and then it's back there—the old burden, the old suffering, the old emptiness, the old monotony, the old grind. Jesus Christ is the only One who can give "the peace that passeth all understanding."

The simple fact is: there can be no real peace in the world until we have peace with God.

The motto of the Apollo II flight was, "We come in peace for all mankind." This motto was on the plaque which was left there on the surface of the moon, where the astronauts landed on the Sea of Tranquillity. Astronauts Neil Armstrong and Buzz Aldrin found themselves in a wonderfully peaceful place there on the moon. Do you know why? There had never been any humans there before!

Not long after the development of the atomic bomb Albert Einstein declared, "The unleashed power of the atom has changed everything except our way of thinking. We shall require a substantially new manner of thinking if mankind is to survive." Later a photographer who had noted the look of immense sadness on Einstein's face asked him, "So you don't believe that there will ever be peace?" "No," the great scientist replied. "As long as there will be man, there will be wars."

Peace is more than a mere cessation of hostilities, a momentary halt in a hot or cold war. Rather, it is something positive. It is a specific relationship with God into which a person is brought. It is a spiritual reality in a human heart which has come into vital contact with the Infinite God.

The Bible says: "But now in Christ Jesus ye who sometimes were far off are made nigh by the blood of Christ. For he is our peace, who hath made both one" (Ephesians 2:13, 14).

A Breach Repaired

I saw a painting in England which showed a soldier who had gone to the front to repair the communications lines. The message which was to flow through those lines meant life to hundreds and perhaps thousands of men. He found a breach in the wires but had nothing with which to repair the break. While the enemy shells were bursting around him, he took one broken cable in his left hand and stretching his right hand grasped the other cable and made the connection. The dramatic picture had a one-word title: "Through."

Christ, in His vicarious death on the cross, repaired the breach between God and man. The Bible says: "He is our peace" (Ephesians 2:14). Those who were afar off are made nigh . . . He has made both one. *Through Him alone* we have peace!

Although God has never been humanity's enemy, we by choice became enemies of God. The revolt began in the Garden of Eden, when Adam revolted against God and allied himself with Satan. It was there that the enmity began. It was there that the abysmal breach was made by humanity, by deliberate choice. Enmity and enemy come from the same root.

The history of man has been the record of a futile effort to live happily and peacefully apart from God. When Israel turned from the worship of Jehovah to the worship of idols, she lost her peace, and either fell a prey to other nations or entered a series of wars. Any step away from the true, living God is a step in the direction of strife.

Hitler felt pretty sure of himself when he denounced the Bible and Christianity and tried to create a "pure Aryan" church with a god who bore a striking resemblance to Thor or Woden, the war gods. We are all acquainted with the record of what happened in Germany. A regime which on the surface looked strong enough to conquer the world crumbled and fell swiftly. Today a new Germany has emerged out of the rubble of World War II. In our tours of Germany we have sensed the heart-hunger of these gifted and virile people for a faith which brings peace and not war.

Jesus said: "Blessed are the peacemakers: for they shall be

called the children of God." Notice, He calls for us to be *peacemakers*—not pacifists. There is a world of difference between the two!

Where does peacemaking begin? How can we become peacemakers?

We have pointed out that peace can never come out of war. War is the sire of poverty, depression, suffering, and hatred—it has never given us permanent peace.

Can peace be discovered within ourselves? Psychiatry has told us that peace is but a mental attitude. Cast off our phobias, shed our neuroses, and "voila!"—we'll have the coveted peace men long for.

Psychiatry Alone Won't Work

I respect psychiatry and psychology for what they can do. One of my sons-in-law is a practicing psychologist and a Christian, and has dedicated his life to helping people who have emotional problems. Many of those problems, he tells me, have a direct relationship to spiritual and moral problems which have caused a person to become insecure and unstable. But emotional stability and peace of mind are no substitute for the lasting inner peace which can only come from God. If psychiatry leaves God out, ultimately we shall see psychiatrists going to each other for treatment. There can be no peace until we find peace with God. The Bible says: "He is our peace" (Ephesians 2:14).

The Bible is not content to leave the nature of the peace Christ purchased for us in doubt. It sketches that peace in the clearest of outlines. Christ made peace by the blood of His cross (Colossians 1:20). He bore the sins of all, so those who know His saviorhood need be troubled by them no longer. He interposed Himself between doomed humanity and the wrath of God. And He stands still between the Holy God and fallen man in his strife, rebellion, and conflict. He is the only hope for peace in the inner spiritual warfare of the soul, and for that reason also is the only hope for social stability.

In a materialistic world which has tried to sever diplomatic relations with God, we have nowhere to retreat except within ourselves. We are like turtles in a traffic jam—the best we can do is to pull our heads back into our shells and shut our eyes. But that's a good way to get the life crushed out of you, as any dead turtle can attest.

Where Does It Begin?

Where does peacemaking begin? How can we become peace-makers in our broken, nervous, frightened, and dangerous world?

If we are to be peacemakers, we first must make our peace with God.

The Bible says: "There is no peace, saith the Lord, unto the wicked" (Isaiah 48:22). The same prophet said: "The way of peace they know not; and there is no judgment in their goings: they have made them crooked paths: whosoever goeth therein shall not know peace" (Isaiah 59:8).

Man's conflict with man has been but an expression on the human level of his conflict against God. Until we find an armistice with God, we cannot know peace among ourselves. Both ancient and modern men have discovered the peace of God. David said: "I will both lay me down in peace, and sleep: for thou, Lord, only makest me dwell in safety" (Psalm 4:8).

A former unbeliever, having recently discovered the peace of God, said to me some years ago, "My wife and I used to wake up in the morning quarreling and go to bed at night bickering—but since we have found peace with God, our home is a heaven on earth."

We can have peace with God! "But how can we discover this peace?" you ask.

A Ceasefire Needed

The first step in finding peace with God is to stop fighting Him. Through the Bible, through the church, through the lives of Christian people, God has been trying to get through to us for years with the message that He wants to give us peace. Christ said to His disciples: "My peace I give unto you" (John 14:27). He is no respecter of persons—He wants to give us peace. But He can't give us His peace as long as we lift high the red flag of rebellion. We must stop resisting God! We must no longer shut Him out of our lives! We must stop fighting! We must give up!

The Solace of Surrender

The second step in finding peace with God is to surrender to Him. We must put down our weapons of war! We must get off the offensive, and stop *being* offensive! The Bible says regarding a people who had no peace with God: "Be ye not stiffnecked, as your fathers were, but yield yourselves unto the Lord" (2 Chronicles 30:8).

When we surrender to a "friendly enemy"—to One who loves us—we are using good sense.

The peace which follows the acceptance of Christ as Savior is more than earthly peace, and it is the greatest of spiritual treasures even though it may not always bring worldly prosperity with it. To know Christ is to have the supremest of riches, a place in the kingdom of God. And men and women who give Him first place find that there is no need for anxiety about this world's goods. "Seek ye first the kingdom of God . . . and all these things shall be added unto you" (Matthew 6:33).

But there is one more aspect of this peace with God. It is not just a passive peace which sits idly under a willow tree strumming a harp. It is a peace of activity and service.

The Secret of Service

The third step in finding peace with God is to serve Him. The Bible told an ancient people who sued for peace not only to yield but to "serve the Lord your God, that the fierceness of his wrath may turn away from you" (2 Chronicles 30:8).

In all of life there is nothing more wonderful than discovering peace with God. Step one to this discovery is realizing God's plan—peace and life. God loves you and wants you to experience peace and life—abundant and eternal.

The Bible says," . . . we have peace with God through our Lord Jesus Christ" (Romans 5:1). John 3:16 says, "For God so loved the world, that he gave his only begotten Son, that whosoever believeth in him should not perish, but have everlasting life." In John 10:10 Jesus said, ". . . I am come that they might have life, and that they might have it more abundantly."

Since God planned for us to have peace, and the abundant life right now, why are most people not having this experience? Step two is acknowledging man's problem—separation. God created man in His own image and gave him an abundant life. He did not make him as a robot to automatically love and obey Him, but gave him a will and freedom of choice. Man chose to disobey God and go his own willful way. Man still makes this choice today. This results in separation from God.

The Bible says, "For all have sinned, and come short of the glory of God" (Romans 3:23). In Romans 6:23 the apostle Paul says, "For the wages of sin is death (separation from God); but the gift of God is eternal life through Jesus Christ our Lord." Man through the ages has tried to bridge this gap in many ways without success.

There is only one remedy for this problem of separation. Step three is recognizing God's remedy—the cross. Jesus Christ is the *only* answer to this problem of separation. When Jesus Christ died on the cross and rose from the grave, He paid the penalty for our sin and bridged the gap from God to man. His *death* and *resurrection* make a new life possible for all who believe.

"God is on one side and all the people on the other side, and Christ Jesus, himself man, is between them to bring them together" (1 Timothy 2:5, *The Living Bible*).

The Bible says, "But God commendeth (showed) his love toward us, in that, while we were yet sinners, Christ died for us" (Romans 5:8). John writes, "Jesus saith unto him, I am the way, the truth, and the life: no man cometh unto the Father, but by me" (14:6). Paul says, "For by grace are ye saved through faith; and that not of yourselves; it is the gift of God: not of works, lest any man should boast" (Ephesians 2:8, 9).

God has provided the only way . . . Man must make the choice. Step four is for man to make his response to receive Christ. We must trust Jesus Christ and *receive Him* by personal invitation. The Bible says, "Behold I stand at the door, and knock (Christ is speaking): if any man hear my voice, and open the door, I will come in to him" (Revelation 3:20). "But as many as received him, to them gave he power to become the sons of God, even to them that believe on his name," writes the apostle John (1:12).

Is there any good reason why you cannot receive Jesus Christ right now? You must:

1. *Admit your need (I am a sinner).*

2. *Be willing to turn from your sins (repent).*

3. *Believe that Jesus Christ died for you on the cross and rose from the grave.*

4. *Through prayer, invite Jesus Christ to come in and control your life. (Receive Him as Lord and Savior.)*

If we take these steps, we have the assurance that ". . . whosoever shall call upon the name of the Lord shall be saved" (Romans 10:13). If we sincerely ask Jesus Christ to come into our lives, we have this promise: "He that hath the Son hath life (right now); and he that hath not the Son of God hath not life. These things have I written unto you that believe on the name of the Son of God; that ye may *know* that ye have eternal life, and that ye may believe on the name of the Son of God" (1 John 5:12, 13).

Some time ago a Christian workman was fatally injured when he fell from a high scaffolding on a construction job. A minister was called, and when he saw the serious condition of the man, he said, "My dear man, I'm afraid you're dying. I exhort you, make your peace with God!"

"Make my peace with God, sir!" said the man, "Why, that was made nineteen hundred years ago when my Savior paid all my debt upon the cross. Christ *is* my peace, and I do know God—I *do* know God!"

Every person can experience the peace of God through Christ: "For he is our peace" (Ephesians 2:14).

Becoming Peacemakers

To have peace *with* God and to have the peace *of* God is not enough. This vertical relationship must have a horizontal outworking, or our faith is in vain. Jesus said that we were to love the Lord with all our hearts and our neighbor as ourselves. This dual love for God and others is like the positive and negative poles of a battery—unless both connections are made, we have no power. A personal faith is normally useless unless it has a social application. A notable exception would be the thief on the cross and other similar situations.

I once saw a cartoon of a man rowing a boat toward a golden shore labeled "heaven." All around him were men and women struggling in vain to reach the shore and safety, but he was heedless of their peril. He was singing, "I am bound for heaven, hallelujah!" That is not an adequate picture of the Christian life.

If we have peace with God and the peace *of* God, we will become peacemakers. We will not only be at peace with our neighbors, but we will be leading them to discover the source of true peace in Christ.

Christianity increases the scope and area of our lives. It takes us from self-centeredness to multi-centeredness. Conversion takes us from introversion to extroversion.

Our lives take on new dimensions when we find peace with God. To explain this in simpler terms, let us visualize a right-angle triangle sitting on its horizontal base. At the apex or highest point in this triangle write the letter "G," representing God. At the point where the perpendicular line meets the base write the letter "Y," representing you. Then, at the opposite end of the horizontal line write the letter "O," which represents others. There, in geometric form, you have a visual diagram of our relationship with God and man. Our lives (which before we found the peace of God were represented by a single dot of self-centeredness) now take in an area in vital contact with two worlds. Peace flows down from God and out to our fellow men. We become merely the conduit through which it flows. But there is peace in being just a "channel."

Being Peacemakers in the Home

There are many areas of our lives where we can be peacemakers. There is no part of our lives which is not affected by this peace of God which we are to share with others.

FIRST: We can be peacemakers in the *home*.

In a complicated, mechanized age, it is no easy matter to keep the domestic life on an even keel. Modern gadgets, modern transportation and modern social changes have all but revolutionized our domestic life. Families are fragmented. The old-fashioned taffy pulls, Sunday afternoon fun times and family altars seem to have gone out with the horse and buggy.

Many homes today have become little more than dormitories, where the members of the family eat and sleep but otherwise have little communication with each other. One woman wrote me and stated, "Our home is a war zone." Major news magazines carry stories of "latchkey kids," youngsters who come home from school to an empty house, seldom seeing their parents and growing up with little love or discipline. Our society has said, "Get ahead! Do your own thing! Don't worry about anyone else—run your own life!" But in the process family life disintegrates and children grow up emotionally scarred and insecure because they have never known the stability of a happy family

The divorce rate has escalated drastically in recent decades. The home—which is the basic unit of our social structure—continues to disintegrate at an alarming rate, even among Christians. The breaking of the marriage vow is having an effect upon our other social institutions. A chain reaction has set in that could ultimately destroy the nation .

In the marriage ceremony, after the vows are said, the minister solemnly and reverently remarks: "What God hath joined together let no man put asunder." Is not God the party of the third part in a marriage? Should He not be taken into account in the marriage and in the home that emerges from that marriage? If God joins the couple together at the outset, should not His Presence be recognized in the home continually from that point on?

Many homes are in trouble today because God has been left out of the domestic picture. With the continual clash of personalities in a domestic pattern, there must be an integrating force, and the Living God is that Force!

He can give love where there has been hate or indifference. He can make a husband sensitive to the needs of his wife, and the wife sensitive to the needs of her husband—instead of two people constantly clamoring and demanding only to have their own needs met. True self-giving love—the kind God has for us, and the kind He can give us for others—is like a beautiful diamond which sends out flashes of light from its many facets. The Bible gives the most profound and concise summary of love's facets in all of literature: "Love is patient and kind; love is not jealous or boastful; it is not arrogant or rude. Love does not insist on its own way; it is not irritable or resentful; it does not rejoice at wrong, but rejoices in the right. Loves bears all things, believes all things, hopes all things, endures all things" (1 Corinthians 13:4–7, RSV).

A gentleman came to me with a serious domestic problem. He and his wife quarreled violently over trifles. Each blamed the other and the domestic stress had built up to the breaking point. I asked him a question to which I already knew the answer, "Do you and your wife go to church, and do you have family prayer?" He answered that they did neither.

"Your trouble in the home, Mr. B." I said, "is the reflection of your lack of peace with God. Get right with God, and you'll be right with your wife!"

The man did just that. In sincere repentance he confessed his sin to God, and I saw his facial expression change as the peace of Christ came into his heart. The light in his face mirrored the new glow in his soul. A few days later he led his wife to Christ. That home is now a happy one, for Christ is its head.

Many couples think that if they have a more luxurious home, get a better job, or live in a different neighborhood their domestic life will be happier. No! The secret of domestic happiness is to let God, the party of the third part in the marriage contract, have His rightful place in the home. Make peace with Him, and then you can be a real peacemaker in the home.

Peace and Our Community

SECOND: We can be peacemakers in the *community*.

Our society is shot through with slander, libel, and gossip. The strife in many communities is almost unbearable. Here again, the basic cause is a faulty relationship with God.

The Bible says: "The works of the flesh are . . . hatred, variance . . . wrath, strife, seditions . . . envyings" (Galatians 5:19–21). True, we find some of these in the first century community of Christians. Yet "Behold, how they love one another" was the remark of those who observed the unique peace of the Christian society.

How can I be a peacemaker in my community?

The formula is simple: first, I must make my own peace with God, and then I can make peace in the community. The fruit of human nature is discord and bickering; "but the fruit of the Spirit is love, joy, peace, longsuffering, gentleness, goodness, faith, meekness, temperance" (Galatians 5:22, 23).

Our trouble is that we have tried to build a good society without God. In many localities we have taken the Bible out of our schools and God out of our conversation. The result is that decency has disappeared from the community, and bedlam reigns. Peace and decorum will be restored when the individuals in the community give God His proper place once more.

That does not mean it is easy to solve the complex problems that face our communities. But they can be alleviated, and we must not withdraw or refuse to lend our hand in untangling some of the problems and injustices that bring havoc to some communities. Nor must we stand back and let those who peddle evil take over our communities and twist the minds and corrupt the bodies of our young people. Paul spent two years in Ephesus—and the corrupt practices of the magicians and others in that pagan city were reversed. We need more men and women who are willing—for Christ's sake—to become involved in political issues and concerns in their communities, and to be peacemakers in His name.

In regard to racial peace, let me say that for true Christians there is no race problem! The ground is level at the cross and there are no second-rate citizens with God. Admittedly, the problems are great, and will not be solved overnight; but if all people concerned will make sure that they have made their peace with God, it will then be a simpler matter to make peace with each other. If we approach the problem with a vindictive, intolerant, and unChristian attitude, we are destined to failure and disaster.

Peace in the Church

THIRD: We can be peacemakers in the *church*.

We might as well face it: strife has even infiltrated our church life. It is true enough that the church is now the church militant. But as such its warfare ought to be that of dedication to revealed truth and divine holiness, and not internal bickering and carnal disputes.

We read in the second chapter of Luke that Joseph and Mary lost Jesus one day. Where did they lose Him? They lost Him in the most unlikely place in all the world—in the temple. Strange, I know! But, I have seen many people lose Jesus right in church. I have seen them lose Him in a dispute about who was to be choir director, who was to play the organ, who was to be an elder, or who was to be the minister. Yes, because we are human, though Christian, it is easy to lose sight of Jesus right in the temple!

I know of two deacons who had quarreled over an old line fence, and they had not spoken to each other for a long time. One of them, wanting to make peace, took his Bible and went to visit his neighbor. Handing his Bible to his "old enemy," he said, "John, you read and I'll pray. We must be friends."

But John, fumbling for his glasses, said, "But I can't read. I haven't my spectacles."

"Take mine," said his peace-loving neighbor.

After they had read the Word and prayed together, they arose and embraced each other. John handed back the spectacles to his neighbor and said through his tears, "Jim, that old line fence looks different through your glasses."

When we have the peace of God, we can see things through "the other man's glasses," and by doing that we can make peace.

Working for Peace at Our Work

FOURTH: We can be peacemakers at *work*.

One of the greatest points of tension in our economy is the labor-management relationship. Many industries today are recognizing that disputation is costly on the part of both labor and management and are seeking industrial peace through God and faith in Him.

One minister wrote us the other day and said that he was chaplain in three industrial plants in Indiana. The managers had found that if they sat down with their employees and listened to the Christian message once each day that everyone was in a better frame of mind.

In London, an industrialist gave his heart to Christ. He wrote us that he now conducts a chapel service in his plant and that two hundred attend the service regularly. "Never has there been more peace in our factory," he wrote.

Would you like to be an industrial peacemaker? You can be one—whether manager or laborer—if you make your peace with God first, and then seek by His grace to impart this peace to others.

When an employer and employees really know Christ, the lie is given to the Marxist thesis that an opiate religion is for the common people. To know Christ is to have part in His saviorhood and Lordship of life. Godlier employers and godlier employees will find that the right makes a claim upon every life. Where the employer is Christ's servant and the employee is the employer's spiritual partner, they are linked in an eternal vocation.

Peacemaking in Our World

FIFTH: We need peacemakers on the *international scene,* also. Many years ago President Eisenhower knelt in a chapel in Geneva before the Big Four Conference and asked God for divine guidance in the deliberations to follow. I believe that God heard and answered, for President Eisenhower during those days displayed the spirit of a true peacemaker on the international level. Kind, considerate of the opposition's viewpoint, and given to intelligent discussion, he emerged the undisputed hero of the Geneva Conference. This was not because he held a "big stick" but because he convinced the others, at least in a measure, that he wanted peace and not war.

Several years ago I was invited to Moscow to attend an international conference of religious leaders to discuss the subject of world peace. It had been called by Patriarch Pimen, the head of the Russian Orthodox Church. At first I was reluctant to go, knowing that my presence might be misunderstood or I might be accused of being naive or manipulated by Soviet authorities. But after much prayer and thought I went, and one reason was my recollection of Jesus' words: "Happy are the peacemakers." I went as an observer and also as a speaker, delivering an address to the entire conference on "The Biblical Meaning of Peace." Later a leading western political figure told me, "At first I thought you were wrong to go. But you were right. We must take risks for peace, because the world is too dangerous unless we learn to listen and talk to each other."

As I made clear in Moscow, I am not a pacifist, nor am I for unilateral disarmament; nations have the right to defend themselves against aggressors. Nor am I naive about the very real problems and barriers that exist between nations of different ideologies. But we must do all we can to work for peace, in whatever ways are open to us.

Is it really possible, however, for a single individual to have any impact in a world which often seems out of control? Certainly! First, encourage those who are leaders to seek peace. Second, pray for peace. The Bible commands, "I exhort therefore, that, first of all, supplications, prayers, intercessions, and giving of thanks, be made for all men; For kings, and for all that are in authority; that we may lead a quiet and peaceable life in all godliness and honesty. For this is good and acceptable in the sight of God our Savior" (1 Timothy 2:1–3). The Bible also reminds us, "The effectual fervent prayer of a righteous man availeth much" (James 5:16).

The only corrective measure in establishing peace is for men as individuals to know the peace of God. Though I am not averse to movements which strive in one way or another for world peace, I have a strong conviction that such peace will never come unless there is a spiritual dynamic at the core. I pray for wars to cease just as I pray for crime to stop; but I know that the basic cause of both crime and war is the inherent sinfulness of human nature.

When Jesus told Nicodemus that he "must be born again," He was addressing not only this great Jewish teacher but all of us, for He saw in Nicodemus a typical representative of the race. The world cannot be reborn until men are born again and are at peace with God.

James asked, "From whence come wars and fightings among you? Come they not hence, even of your lusts that war in your members?" (James 4:1).

Peacemaking is a noble vocation. But you can no more make peace in your own strength than a mason can build a wall without a trowel, a carpenter build a house without a hammer or an artist paint a picture without a brush. You must have the proper equipment. To be a peacemaker, you must know the Peace-Giver. To make peace on earth, you must know the peace of heaven. You must know Him who "is our peace."

Jesus didn't leave a material inheritance to His disciples. All He had when He died was a robe, which went to the Roman soldiers; His mother, whom He turned over to His brother John; His body, which He gave to Joseph of Arimathea; and His spirit, which returned to His Father.

But Jesus willed His followers something more valuable than gold, more enduring than vast land holdings and more to be desired than palaces of marble—He willed us His peace. He said: "My peace I give unto you: not as the world giveth, give I unto you. Let not your heart be troubled, neither let it be afraid" (John 14:27).

Only as we know Him and the peace He imparts can we be peacemakers . . . and He promised happiness to a maker of peace!

The key is commitment to become peacemakers—to be men and women who actively seek to bring the peace of Christ to others and to our world.

Blessed are they which are persecuted for righteousness' sake for theirs is the kingdom of heaven. Matthew 5:10

CHAPTER NINE

Happiness in Spite of Persecution

WHO WANTS to be persecuted? We cannot see happiness in persecution. No one enjoys being maligned. Almost all of us want the good will of our neighbors, and it is difficult to see what blessedness there could be in the enmity of others.

Offhand, it would seem that being a Christian should elicit the admiration and acclaim of those about us. A Christian is usually one who lives his life with kindness, honesty, and unselfishness. Such a person should be blessed, not blasted, it would seem. His peers should stand around him and sing, "For he's a jolly good fellow, which nobody can deny!"

It would seem so! But such is not the case. And it is good that this Beatitude gives us the occasion to sit down and rethink this age-old question: "Why are good people persecuted?" Or as a modern-day author has asked, "Why do bad things happen to good people?"

We Are Not Exempt

A Christian was released from a country that had a hostile regime. He eventually got a job working with Christians. He was asked one day how it had felt to be persecuted for his faith. With a surprised look he said, "We thought it was the normal Christian life."

You may have concluded, as have others, that there is usually something wrong with those who are persecuted for righteousness' sake, that there is some quirk in their disposition, some personality peculiarity or some religious fanaticism which causes others to mistreat them. No, that is not always, or let us say that is not usually, the case.

Nowhere does the Bible teach that Christians are to be exempt from the tribulations and natural disasters that come upon the world. It does teach that the Christian can face tribulation, crisis, calamity and personal suffering with a supernatural power that is not available to the person outside of Christ. Christiana Tsai, the Christian daughter of a former governor of Kiangsu Province in China, wrote, "Throughout my many years of illness (53), I have never dared to ask God why He allowed me to suffer for so long. I only ask what He wants me to do." St. Augustine wrote, "Better is he that suffereth evil than the jollity of him that doeth evil."

The eagle is the only bird which can lock its wings and wait for the right *wind*. He waits for the updraft and never has to *flap* his wings, *just soar. So as we wait* on God He will help us use the adversities and strong winds to *benefit us!* The Bible says, "They that wait upon the Lord . . . shall mount up with wings as eagles" (Isaiah 40:31).

Christians can rejoice in the midst of persecution because they have eternity's values in view. When the pressures are on, they look beyond their present predicament to the glories of heaven. The thought of the future life with its prerogatives and joys helps to make the trials of the present seem light and transient. ". . . for theirs is the kingdom of heaven."

Christians in the People's Republic of China are an illustration of blessings under persecution. In 1949 when the missionaries were forced to leave, there were approximately 700,000 Christians in China. In the beginning, landowners, the educated and Christians were marked for elimination. Of these three categories, which increased in spite of persecution? Those who were "persecuted for righteousness' sake." Today, reliable estimates range from 30 million to 50 million Christians in China.

The early Christians were able to experience joy in their hearts in the midst of persecution. They counted suffering for Christ not as a burden or misfortune but as a great honor, as evidence that Christ counted them worthy to witness for Him through suffering. They never forgot what Christ Himself had gone through for their salvation, and to suffer for His name's sake was regarded as a gift rather than a cross.

He Made No False Promises

Jesus Christ spoke frankly to His disciples concerning the future. He hid nothing from them. No one could ever accuse Him of deception. No one could accuse Him of securing allegiance by making false promises.

In unmistakable language He told them that discipleship meant a life of self-denial, and the bearing of a cross. He asked them to count the cost carefully, lest they should turn back when they met with suffering and privation.

Jesus told His followers that the world would hate them. They would be "as sheep in the midst of wolves." They would be arrested, scourged, and brought before governors and kings. Even their loved ones would persecute them. As the world hated and persecuted Him, so they would treat His servants. He warned further, "They will put you out of the synagogue; indeed, the hour is coming when whoever kills you will think he is offering service to God" (John 16:2, RSV).

Many of Christ's followers were disappointed in Him, for in spite of His warning they expected Him to subdue their enemies and to set up a world political kingdom. When they came face to face with reality, they "drew back and no longer went about with him" (John 6:66, RSV). But the true disciples of Jesus all suffered for their faith.

Tacitus, a Roman historian, writing of the early Christian martyrs, said, "Mockery of every sort was added to their deaths. Covered with the skins of beasts, they were torn by dogs and perished, or were nailed to crosses, or were doomed to the flames and burnt, to serve as nightly illumination, when daylight had expired. Nero offered his gardens for the spectacle." How true were the words of Paul to the early Christians. "Through many tribulations we must enter the kingdom of God" (Acts 14:22, RSV).

Bathed Hands in the Blaze

We are told that the martyrs went rejoicing to their deaths, as if they were going to a marriage feast. They bathed their hands in the blaze kindled for them, and shouted with gladness. One early historian, witnessing their heroism, wrote, "When the day of victory dawned, the Christians marched in procession from the prison to the arena as if they were marching to heaven, with joyous countenances agitated by gladness rather than fear."

We are not surprised that the early Christians rejoiced in suffering, since they looked at it in the light of eternity. The nearer death, the nearer a life of eternal fellowship with Christ. When Ignatius was about to die for his faith in A.D. 110 he cried out, "Nearer the sword, then nearer to God. In company with wild beasts, in company with God."

The Christians of the early church believed that "the sufferings of this present time are not worth comparing with the glory that is to be revealed to us" (Romans 8:18, RSV). Thus they could regard present difficulties as of little consequence and could endure them with patience and cheerfulness.

In all ages Christians have found it possible to maintain the spirit of joy in the hour of persecution. In circumstances that would have felled most people, they have so completely risen above them that they actually have used the circumstances to serve and glorify Christ. Paul could write from prison at Rome, "I want you to know, brethren, that what has happened to me has really served to advance the gospel" (Philippians 1:12, RSV).

In our day millions of Christians in our world live in very difficult situations. For some, life is difficult because they are only a tiny minority in societies in which non-Christians predominate, and they may find themselves discriminated against or scorned. For others, however, there is active oppression or even persecution from governments that do not tolerate religious freedom. It has been estimated that more Christians have suffered and died for their faith in this century than in all previous centuries combined.

In mainland China, for example, thousands of Christians were killed and their churches destroyed or plundered under the Cultural Revolution. Indeed, many Christians had to go underground to worship. Recent reports indicate these restrictions now seem to have been relaxed, but religious faith is still not encouraged. The same is true in many other parts of the world. The resurgence of some of the major non-Christian religions has brought new waves of oppression and persecution for many Christian believers.

That Christians make the best citizens, the most faithful and reliable workers, has begun to dawn on only a few. Until it does, these atheistic regimes are the ultimate losers. The persecuted Christians are definitely on the winning side, if not in this world, then most definitely in the one to come.

There is no doubt that the Bible teaches that every believer who is faithful to Christ must be prepared to be persecuted at the hands of those who are enemies of the Gospel. "Indeed all who desire to live a godly life in Christ Jesus will be persecuted," said Paul (2 Timothy 3:12, RSV).

Other Kinds of Persecution

Is persecution, however, only confined to physical torture and death? Or are there other kinds of persecution?

Certainly persecution can take many forms—some of them obvious, but many of them very subtle. We need to realize that a godly person—one who serves Christ, and exhibits purity and integrity in his life—is not necessarily welcomed or admired by those who live differently. They may even react in scorn, or refuse to include a Christian in their social gatherings because his very presence is a rebuke to them. I have known families who disowned a member who took a strong stand for Christ. An employee may find his advancement blocked because a supervisor is prejudiced against Christians. A teenage girl may find herself laughed at because she refuses to join in the immorality of her schoolmates, or a young man may find that his refusal to get involved with alcohol or drugs makes him unpopular with those who do.

But whatever form it takes, the Bible tells us not to give in to the pressures we face, nor are we to lash out at those who oppose us. Instead, we are to do all we can to show Christ's love to them. "Bless them which persecute you: bless, and curse not. . . . Recompense to no man evil for evil. . . . If it be possible, as much as lieth in you, live peaceably with all men. Dearly beloved, avenge not yourselves. . . . if thine enemy hunger, feed him; if he thirst, give him drink; for in so doing thou shalt heap coals of fire on his head. Be not overcome of evil, but overcome evil with good" (Romans 12:14, 17, 18–21).

Patience in Persecution

However, Christ told His disciples that they were not to count it a stroke of affliction when they were reviled and persecuted. Rather, they were to count it as a favor and a blessing. They were to "rejoice, and be exceeding glad" (Matthew 5: 12). Just as Jesus had overcome the world, so they through His grace and strength would overcome the world. Thus they were to be of good cheer. Here is something to contemplate for those who are persecuted: When the godless plot, God laughs (Psalm 2:4; Psalm 37:12, 13). When the godless prosper, don't fret (Psalm 37:7).

They were to be "more than conquerors" (Romans 8:37). They were to rejoice in tribulation (Romans 5:3). When beaten and threatened with worse treatment if they continued to preach Christ, Peter and John departed, "rejoicing that they were counted worthy to suffer dishonor for the name. And . . . they did not cease teaching and preaching Jesus as the Christ" (Acts 5:41–42, RSV).

As we read the Book of Acts we soon realize that persecution and death intensified the joy of the early Christians.

The apostle Paul could write, "With all our affliction, I am overjoyed" (2 Corinthians 7:4, RSV).

In all his sufferings and sorrows Paul experienced a deep, abiding joy. He writes of being "sorrowful, yet always rejoicing" (2 Corinthians 6:10, RSV). With sincerity he declared that for Christ's sake he was "content with weaknesses, insults, hardships, persecutions, and calamities" (2 Corinthians 12:10, RSV).

I have found in my travels that those who keep heaven in

view remain serene and cheerful in the darkest day. If the glories of heaven were more real to us, if we lived less for material things and more for things eternal and spiritual, we would be less easily disturbed by this present life.

In these days of darkness and upheaval and uncertainty, the trusting and forward-looking Christian remains optimistic and joyful, knowing that Christ someday must rule, and "if we endure, we shall also reign with him" (2 Timothy 2:12, RSV). As someone has said, "Patience (*hupomone*) is that quality of endurance that can reach the breaking point and not break."

At the same time I am equally certain that Christians who have spent years at hard labor or in exile, have passed through periods of discouragement—even despair. Those who have had loved ones destroyed have felt deep loss and intense suffering. Victory for such has not come easily or quickly. But eventually the peace of God does come and with it His joy.

An Upside-Down World

Here is a spiritual law which is as unchangeable as the law of gravity: "All that will live godly in Christ Jesus shall suffer persecution" (2 Timothy 3:12).

We must get this fact firmly fixed in our minds: we live in an upside-down world. People hate when they should love, they quarrel when they should be friendly, they fight when they should be peaceful, they wound when they should heal, they steal when they should share, they do wrong when they should do right.

I once saw a toy clown with a weight in its head. No matter what position you put it in, it invariably assumed an upside-down position. Put it on its feet or on its side, and when you let go it flipped back on its head.

In our unregenerate state we are just like that! Do what you may with us, we always revert to an upside-down position. From childhood to maturity we are always prone to do what we should not do and to refrain from doing what we ought to do. That is our nature. We have too much weight in the head and not enough ballast in our hearts so we flip upside down when left alone.

That is why the disciples to the world were misfits. To an upside-down man, a right-side-up man seems upside down. To the nonbeliever, the true Christian is an oddity and an abnormality. A Christian's goodness is a rebuke to his wickedness; his being right side up is a reflection upon the worldling's inverted position. So the conflict is a natural one. Persecution is inevitable.

When Christ's disciples began preaching that Jesus was the Christ, the people cried in consternation, "These that have turned the world upside down are come hither also" (Acts 17:6). Herein lies the fundamental reason for Christian persecution. Christ's righteousness is so revolutionary and so contradictory to man's manner of living that it invokes the enmity of the world.

If we could assume that people were basically upright, then it would be the popularly accepted thing to "live godly in Christ Jesus" (2 Timothy 3:12). But as long as Satan is loose in the world and our hearts are dominated by his evil passions, it will never be easy or popular to be a follower of Christ.

The Bible says: "But ye are a chosen generation, a royal priesthood, an holy nation, a peculiar people; that ye should show forth the praises of him who hath called you out of darkness into his marvelous light: which in time past were not a people, but are now the people of God: which had not obtained mercy, but now have obtained mercy. Dearly beloved, I beseech you as strangers and pilgrims . . ." (1 Peter 2:9–11).

Aliens are rarely shown the "welcome mat." They are often accepted only with a tongue-in-cheek attitude. Being aliens, with our citizenship not in the world but in heaven, we as Christ's followers will frequently be treated as "peculiar people" and as strangers.

Our life is not of this world. "Our conversation is in heaven" (Philippians 3:20). Our interests, primarily, are not in this world. Jesus said: "Lay up for yourselves treasures in heaven . . . for where your treasure is, there will your heart be also" (Matthew 6:20, 21). Our hope is not in this world. The Bible says: "We look for the Savior, the Lord Jesus Christ: Who shall change our vile body, that it may be fashioned like unto his glorious body, according to the working whereby he is able even to subdue all things unto himself" (Philippians 3:20, 21).

Hence, in every sense we are an enigma to the world. Like a few right-handed persons among a host of left-handed persons, we comprise a threat to their status quo. We cramp their style. We are labeled as "wet blankets," as kill-joys, and as prudes. Like the enemies of Jesus, the world still inquires contemptuously, "Art not thou also one of his disciples?" (John 18:25).

Called Counterfeit

There will be times when the eyes of suspicion will be upon us, because, with people's hearts as they are, they cannot conceive of anyone wanting to live selflessly. Unbelievers will say we have "something up our sleeve," that we have a motive in being so righteous, that it is all a game, that it is sheer hypocrisy. The cry of "counterfeit!" follows the Christian's sincere efforts.

Still another reason for persecution is that there is a war in progress.

The Word of God indicates this! The Bible says: "fight the good fight of faith, lay hold on eternal life" (1 Timothy 6:12). Again: "No man that warreth entangleth himself with the affairs of this life; that he may please him who hath chosen him to be a soldier" (2 Timothy 2:4).

War in the World

The world, the flesh, and the devil are our enemies. In times of war one can hardly expect the good will of the enemy's forces. During World War II the American journalist Cecil Brown wrote a cover story on the tragedy of the sinking of two British battleships, namely, the *Prince of Wales* and *Repulse*. He said, "There is always the danger of underestimating the enemy to the point where you are *over confident*.

Figure him to be *twice* as *good* and *twice* as *smart,* then make preparations in advance!" Though our weapons are not earthly, the enemy's weapons are earthly, and we can expect Satan to use every tool at his command for our persecution and destruction. War atrocities will be committed. They who live godly in Christ *shall* suffer persecution.

All life is a struggle—that is the nature of things. Even within our physical bodies, doctors tell us, a conflict for supremacy is going on. The bacteria in our bloodstream is waging a constant war against alien germs. The red corpuscles fight the white corpuscles constantly in an effort to maintain life within the body. The recent increasingly rampant epidemic of AIDS tragically illustrates this point.

A battle is also raging in the spiritual realm. The Bible says: "We wrestle not against flesh and blood, but against principalities, against powers, against the rulers of the darkness of this world, against spiritual wickedness in high places" (Ephesians 6:12).

"We fight," the Bible says, "against the rulers of the darkness of this world." Darkness hates light. The hymnwriter was writing about war when he asked:

> *Must I be carried to the skies,*
> *On flowery beds of ease;*
> *While others fought to win the prize,*
> *And sailed through bloody seas?*

I once had a dog that would rather have dug up a moldy carcass to chew on than to have the finest, cleanest meal. He couldn't help it—that was his nature.

People cannot help that it is their nature to respond to the lewd, the salacious, and the vile. They will have difficulty doing otherwise until they are born again. And until they *are* changed by the power of Christ, they will likely be at enmity against those who are associated with Christ.

The Cross for Christians

And, finally, Jesus said that a cross is the Christian's lot. "He that taketh not his cross, and followeth after me, is not worthy of me" (Matthew 10:38).

Does this mean that we are to wear a symbol of the cross around our necks or on the lapel of our coats? Or does it mean that we are literally to carry a wooden cross?

No! It means that the reproach of Christ's cross, which He carried when He was in the world, is ours to carry now. Being at "cross-purposes" with the world is part and parcel of the Christian life. We should not covet or expect the praise of ungodly men. On the contrary, we should expect their enmity. The very fact that they are inclined to persecute us is proof that we are "not of the world," that we are "in Christ." All of the persecution, all of the blasphemy, all of the railing that they would heap on Christ, they hurl against us. He took the reproach of the cross for us; now, it is ours to take for Him.

The Privilege of Persecution

As Paul said: "God forbid that I should glory, save in the cross of our Lord Jesus Christ, by whom the world is crucified unto me, and I unto the world" (Galatians 6:14). This, Paul considered a privilege—the privilege of persecution. In that he gloried, because in a small way he was allowed to share in the sufferings of Christ.

Now, let us remember that this Beatitude says: "Blessed are they which are persecuted for righteousness' sake . . . when men shall revile you, and persecute you, and shall say all manner of evil against you falsely . . ." (Matthew 5:10, 11).

Many times we suffer because of our own poor judgment, stupidity and blundering. There is no blessedness in this. I have known professed Christians who were dominated by bad dispositions, snap judgments, and poor manners and thought that people were opposed to them because of their "righteousness." It was not their goodness which people resented—it was their lack of it.

We must be careful not to behave offensively, preach offensively, and dress offensively, and, when people are offended and shun us, blame it on the "offense of the cross." Our personal offensiveness is no credit to the gospel we preach.

Shabby Christians are poor advertisements for Christianity. Paul said: "We . . . suffer reproach, because we trust in the living God . . . but be thou an example of the believers, in word, in conversation, in charity, in spirit, in faith, in purity" (1 Timothy 4:10, 12). The reproach we experience is the natural resentment in the hearts of men toward all that is godly and righteous. This is the cross we are to bear. This is why Christians are often persecuted.

Positive Thoughts on Persecution

We have considered the reasons for Christians being persecuted. Now let us see what happiness and blessedness there
is in persecution. As George MacDonald puts it, we become
"hearty through hardship."

Our Lord instructs the persecuted to be happy. "Rejoice,"
He said, "and be exceeding glad: for great is your reward in
heaven; for so persecuted they the prophets which were before you" (Matthew 5:12).

The word *joy* has all but disappeared from our current
Christian vocabulary. One of the reasons is that we have
thought that joy and happiness were found in comfort, ease,
and luxury. James did not say, "Count it all joy when you fall
into an easy chair," but he said, "Count it all joy when you
fall into divers temptations" (James 1:2).

The persecuted are happy because they are being pro-
cessed for heaven. Persecution is one of the natural conse-
quences of living the Christian life. It is to the Christian what
"growing pains" are to the growing child. No pain, no development. No suffering, no glory. No struggle, no victory. No
persecution, no reward!

The Bible says: "The God of all grace, who hath called us
unto his eternal glory by Christ Jesus, after that ye have
suffered a while, make you perfect, stablish, strengthen, settle
you" (1 Peter 5:10). It is so easy to forget that "all things work
together for good to them that love God" (Romans 8:28).

Jesus, in the Sermon on the Mount, had some commandments for us with regard to our attitude toward persecution.
We are to:

1. *Rejoice and be exceeding glad* (Matthew 5:12)

2. *Love our enemies* (5:44)

3. *Bless them that curse us* (5:44)

4. *Do good to them that hate us* (5:44)

5. *Pray for them that despitefully use us and persecute us* (5:44)

I have a friend who lost his job, a fortune, his wife, and his home. But he tenaciously held to his faith—the only thing he had left. One day he stopped to watch some men doing stonework on a huge church. One of them was chiseling a triangular piece of stone.

"What are you going to do with that?" asked my friend.

The workman said, "See that little opening away up there near the spire. Well, I'm shaping this down here so it will fit in up there."

Tears filled my friend's eyes as he walked away, for it seemed that God had spoken through the workman to explain the ordeal through which he was passing, "I'm shaping you down here so you'll fit in up there."

After you have "suffered a while, make you perfect . . . settle you," echo the words from the Bible.

The persecuted for "righteousness' sake" are happy because they are identified with Christ. The enmity of the world is tangible proof that we are on the right side, that we are identified with our blessed Lord. He said that our stand for Him would arouse the wrath of the world. "And ye shall be hated of all men for my name's sake: but he that endureth to the end shall be saved" (Matthew 10:22).

In a sense, Christ is King in exile, and we who are His followers are often looked upon with derision. To be identified with Him here and now quite naturally entails some "loss of face," some persecution; but some day, we are told, we shall be "kings and priests" and shall be active participators in His kingdom.

Paul must have had this fact in mind when he said: "For I reckon that the sufferings of this present time are not worthy to be compared with the glory which shall be revealed in us. For the earnest expectation of the creature waiteth for the manifestation of the sons of God" (Romans 8:18, 19).

Hope Hangs a Halo

If we should be called upon to suffer all our lives, it would not be long compared to eternity. We are in the position of heirs to a large estate who gladly endure a few days of suffering and privation with the hope that we shall soon come into our fabulous inheritance. Such a glorious hope hangs a halo over the drab existence of the here and now.

Life cannot lose its zest when down underneath our present discomfort is the knowledge that we are children of a King. Complaining becomes foolish; behaving in the manner of the world is unworthy; and love, gentleness, and meekness become the hallmark of God's nobility. "All things" are taken in stride; burdens become blessings in disguise; every wound, like good surgery, is for our good; and etched in every cross is the symbol of a crown.

And last, persecution is blessed because it forms a dark backdrop for the radiance of the Christian life.

The Need for Sunshine and Shadow

All the masterpieces of art contain both light and shadow. A happy life is not one filled only with sunshine, but one which uses both light and shadow to produce beauty. The greatest musicians as a rule are those who know how to bring song out of sadness. Fanny Crosby, her spirit aglow with faith in Christ, saw more with her sightless eyes than most of us do with normal vision. She has given us some of the great gospel songs which cheer our hearts and lives. She wrote some 2,000 hymns of which 60 are still in common use.

Paul and Silas sang their song of praise at midnight in a rat-infested jail in Philippi, their feet in stocks, their backs raw from the jailer's whip. But their patience in suffering and persecution led to the conversion of the heathen prison warden. The blood of the martyrs is mixed well into the mortar which holds the stones of civilization together.

The self-sacrifice of God's people through the centuries has contributed immeasurably to our culture, to our ethics, and to our faith. Down deep we know that there are still things worth dying for, that an existence void of faith is still a fate worse than death.

O children of God, despair not at your suffering and persecution. In the words of Thornton Wilder: "Without your wounds, where would your power be that sends your low voice trembling into the hearts of men? The very angels of

God in heaven cannot persuade the wretched and blundering children of earth as can one human being broken on the wheels of living. In love's service only wounded soldiers will do."

Messages from the Martyrs

Sanders, the martyr, said, "Welcome the cross of Christ. . . . I feel no more pain in the fire than if I were on a bed of down."

Another martyr said, "The ringing of my chain hath been music in my ears; O what a comforter is a good conscience." Kissing the stake, he said, "I shall not lose my life but change it for better; instead of coals I shall have pearls."

You may not be called upon to suffer as the martyrs suffered, for this is an hour when Satan employs psychological warfare. Jesus said: "Men shall revile you . . . and shall say all manner of evil against you falsely, for my sake" (Matthew 5:11). The tongue often inflicts a more painful wound than does the sword. To be laughed at can be harder to take than to be flogged.

Some in reading this may feel that because they are not at present being persecuted, they are not living godly lives. That is not necessarily so. While there are countries where today to be an active Christian is to court death and worse, we live in a predominantly Christian country where active persecution is at a minimum.

Our environment, as well as the age in which we live, has much to do with the amount of persecution a Christian will be called upon to bear. I have known certain overly eager Christians who actually courted persecution for fear that otherwise they would not be living godly enough lives.

Remember, not all Christians are called upon to suffer at all times. Even our Lord increased in wisdom and knowledge and in favor with God and man. But the periods of popularity did not last. It ended on a cross. The important thing is to walk with Christ. Live for Christ! Have one consuming passion in life—to please Him! And let the chips fall where they may. I believe it was Samuel Rutherford who said, "Never take one step out of the pathway of duty either to take a cross or to escape one."

W. C. Burns of India wrote, "Oh, to have a martyr's heart if not a martyr's crown!"

Popularity and adulation are far more dangerous for the Christian than persecution. It is easy when all goes smoothly to lose our sense of balance and our perspective. We must learn like Paul "how to abound" and "how to be abased." We must learn in "whatsoever state" we are "therewith to be content" (Philippians 4:11).

As we have said, the important thing is to walk with Christ, to live for Christ, and to have one consuming passion to please Him. Then, whatever happens, we know that He has permitted it to teach us some priceless lesson and to perfect us for His service. He will enrich our circumstances, be they pleasant or disagreeable, by the fact of His presence with us. The tomorrows fill us with dread. John 10:4 says, "He putteth forth his own sheep." Whatever awaits us is *encountered* first by Him—like the oriental shepherd always went ahead of his sheep—therefore any attack on sheep has to *deal first* with the shepherd—all the *tomorrows* of our lives have to pass Him before they get to us!

Three Hebrew children were cast into the burning fiery furnace, but the king said: "Lo, I *see four* men loose, walking in the midst of the fire, and they have no hurt; and the form of the fourth is like the Son of God" (Daniel 3:25). Our God is with us in the persecution of this life!

A comforting story comes from some unknown writer. The first convert of a certain missionary was tortured to death for his faith. Years later, the missionary too died. In heaven he met that first convert and asked him how it felt to be tortured to death for his faith. "You know," the man replied with a shrug and looking a bit bewildered, "I can't even remember."

CHAPTER TEN

Steps to Happiness

KING GEORGE V wrote on the flyleaf of the Bible of a friend: "The secret of happiness is not to do what you like to do, but to learn to like what you have to do."

Too many think of happiness as some sort of will-o-the-wisp thing that is discovered by constant and relentless searching. Happiness is not found by seeking. It is not an end in itself. Pots of gold are never found at the end of the rainbow, as we used to think when we were children; gold is mined from the ground or panned laboriously from a mountain stream.

Jesus once told His disciples: "Seek ye first the kingdom of God, and his righteousness; and all these things shall be added unto you" (Matthew 6:33). The "things" He spoke of were the basic needs of life: food, drink, clothes, shelter. He told us not to make these the chief goal of our lives but to "seek the kingdom," and these needs would be automatically supplied. And if for some reason only He knows they should be withheld, know that it is for our good and His glory. There have been occasions when Christians have been deprived of one or all these things. They have died of starvation at times—or of thirst or exposure. It is not because He has broken His promise, but because He has something better for us.

There, if we will take it, is the secret of happiness: "Seek ye first the kingdom of God . . . and all . . . shall be added unto you."

Steps to Abundant Living

In the foregoing pages we have tried to interpret Jesus' formula for happiness. We realize that in many ways the interpretation falls short, both in content and clarity. The more we read this introduction to the Sermon on the Mount, the more wisdom we see hidden in it and the more convinced we are if it is read thoughtfully and prayerfully and applied to life that a richer, fuller happiness will ensue.

In summing up the secret of happiness within the framework of the Beatitudes, we would like to suggest several steps to the abundant life:

We must recognize our spiritual poverty. Don't let pride say, "I am rich, and increased with goods, and have need of nothing" (Revelation 3:17). Remember that our own righteousness is as filthy rags and that salvation is not of works but is the gift of God. We must keep ever in mind the first Beatitude: "Blessed are the poor in spirit: for theirs is the kingdom of heaven."

God measures people by the small dimension of humility and not by the bigness of their achievements or the size of their capabilities.

We must make sure we have received Christ. Remember, it is not creeds, culture, or even respectability that saves us. It is Christ. The Bible says: "But as many as received him, to them gave he power to become the sons of God, even to them that believe on his name" (John 1:12).

Let us say that one day you decided to go to Europe on a jet plane. Perhaps you might contact your travel agency and get all kinds of information about flight schedules and the type of plane you would be flying. You might talk with people who had traveled across the Atlantic on that aircraft. You might even have investigated the airline's safety record and become convinced that the pilot and crew were trustworthy and the aircraft would take you safely. You might have said to yourself, *I believe this airplane is able to take me across the Atlantic.* You might even have gotten a ticket and gone to the airport. You might have done all this and still never have crossed the Atlantic. One thing was lacking: you needed to get on the plane—commit yourself to it and trust it to carry you to your destination.

To know about Christ is not enough. To be convinced that He is the Savior of the world is not enough. To affirm our faith in Him, as we do in the Apostles' Creed, is not enough. To believe that He has saved others is not enough. We really don't actively believe in Christ until we make a commitment of our lives to Him and receive Him as Our Savior.

We can best demonstrate our faith in a bank by putting

our money in it. We can best show our faith in a doctor by trusting him with our physical welfare in times of illness. We can best prove our faith in a boat by getting aboard and going some place on it. We can best demonstrate our faith in Christ by trusting Him with our life and receiving Him unconditionally as our Savior.

We must maintain a contrite spirit. The Bible says: "A broken and a contrite heart, O God, thou wilt not despise" (Psalm 51:17). Remember it was to Christians that John wrote: "If we confess our sins, he is faithful and just to forgive us our sins, and to cleanse us from all unrighteousness" (1 John 1:9).

A cultured person is quick with a courteous apology when he has done wrong. If a gentleman stumbles over a lady's foot in a drawing room, he doesn't wait a week to say, "I beg your pardon!" He begs forgiveness immediately.

When we break God's law, utter a hasty, bitter word, or even think an evil thought, immediately we should confess this sin to God. And in accordance with His Word, He will forgive and cleanse our hearts and transform us into His likeness.

We must be sensitive to the needs of others. In the eternal triangle of Christianity, God is first, others are second, and self is last. "Rejoice with them that do rejoice, and weep with them that weep" (Romans 12:15). We should be sympathetic, tolerant, and understanding. Remember the third secret of happiness: "Blessed are they that mourn: for they shall be comforted."

There is no joy in life like the joy of sharing. Don't be content to have too much when millions in the world have too little. I should remember every time I read the Bible that millions have no Bible to read. We should bear in mind when we hear the gospel preached that more than half the world has never heard the gospel story. Let our lives, our means, and our prayers be shared with those millions who at this moment are wondering whether there is any relief from their distress.

Don't be a half-Christian. There are too many of such in the world already. The world has a profound respect for people who are sincere in their faith.

The Bible tells us that we can't serve God and Mammon, that no man can serve two masters. Too many Christians, so called, are like the little chameleon which adapts its coloration to that of its surroundings. Even a critical world is quick to recognize a real Christian and just as quick to detect a counterfeit.

We must live surrendered lives. The Bible is explicit at this point. It says: "Know ye not, that to whom ye yield yourselves servants to obey, his servants ye are to whom ye obey; whether of sin unto death, or of obedience unto righteousness?" (Romans 6:16).

A friend of David Livingstone once said: "When I watched Livingstone carry out the 'leave all and follow me' life, I became a Christian in spite of myself." The world knows no greater challenge than the surrendered life.

We should be filled with the Spirit. People who have moved the world have been Spirit-filled. Filled with the Spirit, the first disciples "turned the world upside down." Filled with the Spirit, the reformers started the spiritual blaze which became the Reformation. Filled with the Spirit, John and

Charles Wesley, working out of Oxford University, saved a great nation from moral and political collapse. Filled with the Spirit, Francis Asbury, George Fox, Jonathan Edwards, Charles Finney, and David Brainerd set the mountains and prairies of America aglow with the fires of real Christianity. Filled with the Spirit, D. L. Moody and Ira Sankey shook two continents out of their spiritual lethargy. Corrie ten Boom and Mother Teresa impacted their world greatly.

The tides of civilization have risen, the courses of nations have been changed and the pages of history have been brightened by people who have been filled with the Spirit of God.

What does it mean to be filled with the Spirit? It is not necessarily an emotional experience, nor will it necessarily bring us some type of spiritual experience that is obvious or open. *To be filled with the Spirit is to be controlled by the Spirit.* It is to be so yielded to Christ that our supreme desire is to do His will. When we come to Christ the Spirit comes to dwell within us—whether we are aware of His presence or not. But as we grow in Christ, our goal is to be controlled by the Spirit. Have you yielded your life to Christ without reserve, asking Him to fill you and use you for His glory?

We should seek to produce the fruit of the Spirit in our lives. The Bible says: "The fruit of the Spirit is love, joy, peace, longsuffering, gentleness, goodness, faith, meekness, temperance" (Galatians 5:22, 23).

You say, "I am powerless to produce such fruit. It would be utterly impossible for me to do so!"

With that I agree! That is, we can't produce this fruit in our own strength. Remember, the Bible says: "The fruit of the *Spirit* is love, joy, peace, longsuffering, gentleness, goodness, faith, meekness, temperance" (Galatians 5:22–23). When the Spirit of God dwells in us *He* will produce the fruit. It is ours only to cultivate the soil of our hearts through sincere devotion and yieldedness that He might find favorable ground to produce that which He will.

I might have a fruit tree in my yard; but if the soil isn't enriched and the bugs carefully destroyed, it will not yield a full crop.

As Christians, we have the Spirit of God in us. But ours is the responsibility to keep sin out of our lives so that the Spirit can produce His fruit in us.

We must become grounded in the Bible. As Christians, we have only one authority, one compass: the Word of God.

In a letter to a friend, Abraham Lincoln said: "I am profitably engaged in reading the Bible. Take all of this Book upon reason that you can and the balance upon faith, and you will live and die a better man."

Coleridge said he believed the Bible to be the Word of God because, as he put it, "It finds me."

"If you want encouragement," John Bunyan wrote, "entertain the promises."

Martin Luther said, "In Scriptures, even the little daisy becomes a meadow."

The Bible is our one sure guide in an unsure world.

Great leaders have made it their chief Book and their reliable guide. Herbert J. Taylor, formerly international president of Rotary, told me that he began each day by reading the Sermon on the Mount aloud. President Ronald Reagan revered the Bible so much that he proclaimed 1984 the "year of the Bible."

We should begin the day with the Book, and as it comes to a close let the Word speak its wisdom to our souls. Let it be the firm foundation upon which our hope is built.

Let it be the Staff of Life upon which our spirit is nourished. Let it be the Sword of the Spirit which cuts away the evil of our lives and fashions us in His image and likeness.

We must witness for Christ. Jesus said to us: "Ye are the light of the world. Let your light so shine before men, that they may see your good works, and glorify your Father which is in heaven" (Matthew 5:14, 16).

One faithful witness is worth a thousand mute professors of religion.

The late Tom Allan, Scotland's famous preacher, was brought to Christ while a black soldier was singing "Were You There When They Crucified My Lord?" He said it was neither the song nor the voice, but the spirit in which that soldier sang—something about his manner, something about his sincerity of expression—that convicted him of his wicked life and turned him to the Savior.

Our faith grows by expression. If we want to keep our faith, we must share it—we must witness!

We must practice the Presence of God. Jesus said: "Lo, I am with you alway, even unto the end of the world" (Matthew 28:20). Remember, Christ is always near us. We should say nothing that we would not wish to say in His presence. We should do nothing that we would not do in His presence. We should go to no place that we would not go in His presence. But He is not with us just to judge or condemn us; He is near to comfort, protect, guide, encourage, strengthen, cleanse and help. He will not only be with us until the "end of the world," but He will be with us "world without end." He will be with us throughout all eternity.

We must learn the exercise of prayer. Jesus said: "Men ought always to pray, and not to faint" (Luke 18:1). He said on another occasion: "Pray to thy Father which is in secret; and thy Father which seeth in secret shall reward thee openly" (Matthew 6:6).

Prayer is not just asking. It is listening for God's orders. The late Frank Laubach said: "Prayer at its highest is a two-way conversation; and for me, the most important part is listening to God's replies."

The world's great Christians have set regular hours for prayer. John Wesley arose at four in the morning and started the day with prayer, followed by an hour's Bible study.

I suggest an established time for communication with God. Make a date with Him and keep it. The Christian will never regret such a practice, for the "fervent prayer of a righteous man availeth much" (James 5:16).

We must develop a taste for spiritual things. "Happy are they which do hunger and thirst after righteousness: for they shall be filled."

Spiritual tastes, like physical tastes, can be cultivated. I didn't always like yogurt, but they told me that it was good for me, so I kept trying to like it—and now I enjoy it.

It will not perhaps be easy at first to read the Bible, witness, and pray. But after we experience the strength that can come from these means of grace, they will become part of our routine, as much as breathing and eating. These are the things that give strength to the soul.

We must not be critical of others. Habitual criticism can stifle our spiritual growth. We must not build up ourselves at the expense of others. If I praise others, then others will praise me. But if I condemn others, they in turn will condemn me. Criticism begets criticism, but praise begets praise. As Jesus said: "Happy are the merciful: for they shall obtain mercy."

We must not be envious of others. Two of the most devastating sins of today are envy and covetousness. Envying others can work havoc in our spiritual lives and sap us of our spiritual strength. It can also ruin our social batting average and weaken our Christian testimony. We must not be enslaved by this ruinous evil! It can destroy our happiness and rob our lives of their sweetness.

We should love everybody. The Bible says: "Let love be genuine; hate what is evil, hold fast to what is good" (Romans 12:9, RSV). This Scripture says: *"Let* love," as if it were possible for us to hinder love from being all that it should be. The love of Christ, if unhindered and unblocked by our prejudices and our malices, will embrace everyone. Christ in us will go on loving even the unlovely if He is not hindered by our selfishness. We must realize the difference between loving the sinner while hating his sin.

We should stand courageously for the right. Horace Pitkin, the son of a wealthy merchant, was converted and went to China as a missionary. He wrote to his friends in America, saying: "It will be but a short time till we know definitely whether we can serve Him better above or here." Shortly afterward, a mob stormed the gate of the compound where Pitkin defended the women and children. He was beheaded and his head offered at the shrine of a heathen god, while his body was thrown outside in a pit with the bodies of nine Chinese Christians. Sherwood Eddy, writing about him, said: "Pitkin won more men by his death than he ever could have won by his life." The same could be said of the five courageous Christians who died for Christ in Ecuador.

Christ needs people today who are made of martyr stuff! Dare to take a strong, uncompromising stand for Him.

We should learn to relax in Christ. I once watched a little baby learning to walk. As long as it kept its eyes on its mother it was relaxed and in perfect balance. But as soon as it looked down at its little wobbly legs, it failed.

Simon Peter found it possible to walk over the waves of Galilee as long as he kept his eyes on Christ—but when he looked away from the Savior he sank.

These are turbulent times in which we live. People are harassed with tensions, fears, and phobias. Nothing can relieve the tensions of life like a valid faith in Christ.

You, too, can learn to relax in *Christ!*

We must not be victims of paranoia. I am not talking here, of course, about the specific mental illness of paranoia which grips some people and which needs to be treated professionally; I refer here to it in a more general sense. I am talking about an excessive sensitivity to what others say or do about us, which causes us to become overly absorbed in worry and anxiety over what people think about us.

In other words, don't be hypersensitive to criticism or entertain an exaggerated sense of your own importance. This is the secret of unhappiness. Many egocentric people are victims of this terrible disease of the mind. If people never actually criticize them, they at least imagine that they do, and they suffer the agonies of a mental inferno.

Or some people are insecure, lacking in self-confidence, and are therefore easily bruised by what other people say. It may not be easy, but such a person needs to develop more self-confidence by seeing himself the way God sees him. If this is your problem, recognize it for what it is and realize the damage it can cause you. Then ask God to help you overcome it in practical ways.

The paranoid sees two acquaintances talking together somewhat seriously, and immediately he imagines that they are discussing his faults. He retreats into the torture chamber of his own mind where he manufactures misery in wholesale lots. Run from paranoia as you would run from a plague.

We must remember we are immortal and will live forever. To expect absolute, unqualified bliss in this life is expecting a bit too much. Remember, this life is only the dressing room for eternity. In the Beatitudes Jesus said that in this life there are persecution, slander, libel, and deception. But He also said: "Rejoice, and be exceeding glad: for great is your reward in heaven" (Matthew 5:12).

He strongly hinted that relative happiness in this life is related to an absolute happiness in the after life. Here we have an "earnest" of our inheritance, a "down payment," but in heaven we come into our full estate of happiness.

Christians think and act within the framework of eternity. They are not embittered when things don't turn out the way they planned. They know that the sufferings of this present world are not worthy to be compared with the glory that shall be revealed hereafter. So rejoice and be exceedingly glad!

In the covered wagon days when gold was discovered in the Old West, the pioneers endured the sufferings of the prairies, the mountains, and the desert, and the savage attacks of the Indians because they knew that beyond those Sierras lay the promise of gold.

When Bill Borden, son of the wealthy Bordens, left for China as a missionary, many of his friends thought he was foolish to "waste his life," as they put it, trying to convert a few heathen to Christianity. But Bill loved Christ and he loved people! On his way to China he contracted a disease and died. At his bedside they found a note that he had written while he was dying. It read: "No reserve, no retreat, and no regrets."

Borden had found more happiness in his few years of sacrificial service than most people find in a lifetime.

Many thousands of rational, cultured citizens of the earth have found happiness in Christ. You can too! But, remember, you will never find it by searching directly for it. As the Lord of happiness said: "Seek ye first the kingdom of God, and his righteousness; and all these things shall be added unto you" (Matthew 6:33).